RETAIL BANKING TECHNOLOGY

Retail Banking Technology
Strategies and Resources That Seize the Competitive Advantage

Michael Violano
and
Shimon-Craig Van Collie

JOHN WILEY & SONS, INC.
New York • Chichester • Brisbane • Toronto • Singapore

This publication is designed to provide accurate and authoritative information in regard to the subject matter covered. It is sold with the understanding that the publisher is not engaged in rendering legal, accounting, or other professional services. If legal advice or other expert assistance is required, the services of a competent professional person should be sought. *From a Declaration of Principles jointly adopted by a Committee of the American Bar Association and a Committee of Publishers.*

Library of Congress Cataloging-in-Publication Data

Violano, Michael.
    Retail banking technology: strategies and resources that seize the competitive advantage / by Michael Violano and Shimon-Craig Van Collie.
    p. cm.
    Includes index.
    ISBN 0-471-53174-X (acid-free paper)
    1. Banks and banking—United States—Customer service. I. Van Collie, Shimon-Craig. II. Title.
HG1616.C87V55   1992
    332.1'068'8—dc20   92-10079

10 9 8 7 6 5 4 3 2 1

Acknowledgments

Many people contributed their thoughts, talents, time, and support to this book.

The insights and leading-edge leadership of bankers was perhaps the greatest contribution and a source of constant inspiration. After all, banking technology arises from those who take the chances and practice what they preach daily. Among the many, those whose wisdom and accomplishments in retail banking merit special mention are Edward Cruthfield, Michael Zucchini, David VanLear, John McCoy, Hugh McColl, Michael Bal, Vern Canfield, Bob Goddard, Linda Lockhart, Dick Gallerno, Mark Hodson, and Rex Johnson. Countless others, too numerous to name here, are credited throughout the book.

Champions of bank technology—the creators of the systems and software—were also essential in helping to craft the words on these pages. We extend a special credit to the contributions and participation of Phil Sonnenberg, John Cook, Robert Parks, Don Crosbie, Dorothy Botnick, Frank Sanchez, Kathleen Archambeau, Glenn LaFrank, Bill Bradley, Cynthia Stine, Bing Michael, and Pete Van Sistine.

The staff at *Bankers Monthly* provided both encouragement and the "opportunity to write and be read" during the project. We extend our appreciation to Annette Gonella, Robert Bruce Slater, Elaine Kursch, and Lynne Winters.

We owe a very special debt to Wendy Grau, our editor, who spent months of effort to make the book reach you. In addition to cheerleading and challenging us, Wendy helped to structure our thinking and straighten our writing. No easy task.

Shimon also thanks those who assisted in making his research easier, including Tom Pritzker, Arlene Gleicher, Roberta Edwards, Mike Rubin, Paco Underhill, Richard D'Agostino, Donna Stockton, Jekka Ashman, Kathy Fowler, Debbie Bevier, Leora Zahorik, Phil Carter, Jim McGovern, Greg Berardi, Russ Yarrow, Charles Conway, Randi Long, and Mel Strauss.

Also, for their support in helping Shimon keep his promises, he thanks Paul Hirschberger and Kimberly Call.

Thanks to our wives and partners, Alison Violano and Katrina LaThrop-Van Collie; respectively and respectfully, we say: Without you, our work would mean much, much less. And a special thanks from Michael to daughters Leila and Maya and sister Beverly Earle, who never stopped believing or encouraging.

Preface

Generalizations are often stale and stereotypical. However, it is probably safe to say that senior retail bank executives are strategic, individualistic, and opportunistic in their approach to managing. And, over the course of their careers, they have earned the right to a personal style of leadership, as long as it profits the bank.

But why do bank senior executives fear computers and technology? Perhaps it is because they are afraid to appear lacking in skills demanded of others, or maybe (as many claim) they just don't have the time to learn, or they fail to see how such systems can help them in their own decision-making and strategy-setting. When you probe deeper, you find the root causes of computer fear go far beyond keyboard-phobia.

Bank executives distrust automation.

Information technology is at the heart of Great Western Financial Corporation's modern success story. In a recent speech, James Montgomery, CEO of Great Western, pondered the high-tech dilemma: "How does our dependence on the computer look to me? Sometimes it looks exciting. Sometimes it looks frightening. And sometimes it just looks expensive."

In *Technology Investments: Maximizing Value in Banks*, a report prepared by Andersen Consulting in conjunction with Bank Administration Institute, researchers concluded: "With several decades behind them, many bankers lack confidence in the wisdom or effectiveness of their technology investments. Most are . . . somewhat skeptical about any true payoff."

The truth is that thousands of retail banks have dismally failed to reap the elusive gains in profit and productivity that technology has promised. Technology in banking has always been considered a two-edged sword—a risk and an opportunity, a trick and a treat. Sigmund Freud knew a thing or two about technology and its effect on individuals—from leaders to laborers. In *Civilization and Its Discontents*, Freud observed, "Man has become a kind of prosthetic god. When he puts on all his auxiliary organs he is truly magnificent; but those organs have not grown on him and they still give him trouble at times."

Technologists miss the point in all the confusion and debate about computer-literate bank executives and CEOs. The issue is not computer literacy, it is *information literacy*. The real challenge facing retail bank executives in the 1990s is customer information literacy. Banks have so many data; the systems in place for transaction processing are "factory" systems—they are not information systems.

Technology runs through the bank like electricity in a house. It is everywhere, a vital and powerful resource. But unlike electricity, technology in banking is ever-changing, advancing, creating new opportunities to bring the bank closer to the customer.

Before you begin, take pen or marker in hand. We intend this to be a dialog. Interact with the book. Mark it up; discuss critical issues with your colleagues. And if you are moved or puzzled, write to us; we will respond.

Michael Violano, Teaneck, New Jersey
Shimon-Craig Van Collie, Berkeley, California

Contents

Introduction: A Call to Action   **1**

The Keys of the Kingdom, 2
The "Cs" of Success, 3
No Simple Answers, 6

1 Relationship Banking for The 21st Century   **9**

Bank ID, 10
A Ken for Customers, 19
The Quest to Provide Quality Service, 27

2 Information and Integration   **31**

Customer Information Resources, 32
Care and Maintenance of Information Systems, 38
MIS vs End Users: Forging a Truce in the Technology
Tug-of-War, 43

3 Teller System and Service Imperatives   **51**

Facts and Figures, 51
Teller Automation Renaissance, 54
Service Par Excellence, 60

4 The Promise of Platform Automation   67

Risks and Rewards, 67
Platform Dilemmas, 75
Bringing It All Together, 77

5 Electronic Banking   83

The Rebirth of the ATM, 83
Automated Voice Response, 92
Debit Cards and Point-of-Sale Strategies, 102

6 Innovative Imaged Products and Services   107

First Encounters with Image, 108
Taming the Paper Tiger, 108
Fleeting Images of Check Processing, 115
Payoffs and Pitfalls, 118

7 Marketing Systems and Strategies   123

The Marketer's Mission, 123
Research and Planning, 125
Marketing CIFs, 127
Database Marketing, 131
Direct Contact and Telemarketing, 134

8 Sales and Staff Performance   139

Sales Culture Shock, 139
Sales Reporting Systems, 143
Reward Performance, 147
All Aboard the Training Express, 151

9 Branch Bank Merchandising   157

Bank Retailing, 158
Branches as Communication and Media Centers, 163
Branches of the Future, 168

10 Breaking Banking Barriers   175

> Supermarket Branching, 177
> Banks Without Walls, 182
> Technology That Breaks Through Barriers, 186
> Swift and Sure Communication Networks, 190

11 Productivity and Profitability   195

> Productivity: The Elusive Goal, 195
> Systems Support Success, 202
> The Rocky Road of Risk Management, 206

Subject Index   213

Bank Company Index   221

Introduction:
A Call to Action

Retail bankers were roughed up in the 1980s. And most bank watchers expect the 1990s to be a devastating decade for the nation's financial institutions both large and small. Why? Well, the commercial real estate debacle that gutted the Southwest has spread across the country; Northeastern banks have been left holding the bad land loan bag and the epidemic is affecting the Middle Atlantic, Southeastern, and Western states. While the worst of the savings and loan crisis is over, lingering problems persist, affecting both banks and thrifts. The legacy of mismanaged savings institutions and the robber barons of banking will be borne by the American taxpayer and the banks that survive.

Bank earnings are a fragile thing. The slightest tilt in the economy or a bad cold in the credit portfolio can put an otherwise healthy bank on the skids, with shareholder value following closely behind. Recession and stagflation spell trouble for bankers as the decade begins. Who will step forward to save the banks?

Some look to government. Bankers clamor for repeal of the last remaining restrictions of FDR's aging Glass-Steagall Act. But legislators fear that more freedom will result in license to lose more money. Witness the more stringent capital requirements for banks that have already gone into effect and expect the seesaw of deregulation and reregulation to continue.

Some believe that size favors large financial institutions with economies of scale. Sheer size, as measured by assets, does not connote strength. Big is good, but better is better. In 1989, only five of the top ten banks in assets were among the top ten net income earners; only Wells Fargo Bank, a retail banking giant, made the list of the top ten banks in return on equity (ROE).

Some seek growth. However, in *Analyzing Success and Failure in Banking Consolidation*, researchers from FMCG Capital Strategies and the Bank Administration Institute critiqued the consolidation phenomenon in banking. They found that many acquisition-hungry banks, in the billion-plus asset class, had a case of indigestion leading to earnings stagnation and, in turn, became easy targets of other acquirers. Only a handful of multiple acquiring banks, including NationsBank, Banc One, and Fleet Norstar, have mastered the art of territorial expansion.

Bankers who have seen bad days counsel a good defense for troubling times. They are the caretakers who institute "prevent offense" policies to avoid mistakes. They delay or curtail technology investments and jettison unwanted assets. The risk: Those who go slowly are likely to be passed.

Others see technology as the savior. Banker beware: Leading-edge automation does not automatically correlate with success, although it has become a necessary attribute to compete. The chasm between the banks that have technological resources and power and those that do not is widening. Baseline automation barely ensures survival.

THE KEYS OF THE KINGDOM

The aim of this book is to reveal the tactics and strategies that bankers can and do employ to realign their retail banking organizational structure with strategic plans and technological resources for profit and gain. Two components emerge as essential—the customer and information.

If anyone or anything is to save the retail banking industry it is the customer. Some bankers have a slight edge already, they are courting customers at every contact. However, opportunities abound for all as long as bankers admit their weaknesses and remake their organizations. The best starting point is to assess the situation as it stands.

Customer confidence in retail banking reached an all-time low as the gun sounded the start of the 1990s. In the airline industry, a carrier is only as good as the customer's most recent flight; in banking, an institution is only as good as its last contact with the customer. Today's bankers cannot assume customer loyalty. Bankers cannot take customers for granted nor can they rely on customer inertia. Many customers will walk next door or down the street for better service. As time goes on, expect customers to switch to bank and nonbank financial providers who happen to be headquartered across the country, or even on the other side of the world.

If bankers are to make the transformation from passive, account-holding, transaction-processing institutions to aggressive, opportunistic, customer-focused, service-oriented organizations, there are many changes to implement.

THE "Cs" OF SUCCESS

Change

The financial industry has experienced more political, economic, and technological change in the last generation than in the century that preceded it. Change is not a concept or an action that is warmly embraced by bank executives, particularly CEOs. Change involves risk. Change demands questioning (and at least a partial rejection of) the status quo. There are some who would say that change in banking occurs at the rate of continental drift, but that seems a bit harsh.

Bankers need a healthy openness to change, a questioning, critical mind-set. A clean slate helps to consider alternatives and test new ideas, products, and approaches. Many innovators preach a path to discovery that will position the institution apart from the crowd. Differentiation is most desirable.

Consider the "McBanking" phenomenon—superregional retail banks with a knack for profitable, prenational expansion. Charlotte-based NationsBank (formerly NCNB) under the leadership of CEO Hugh McColl, and Chairman John McCoy's Banc One empire, headquartered in Columbus, Ohio, are the foremost examples. These institutions began the decade of the 1980s as respectable retail banks, well known to the customers in their home state. After scores of out-of-state acquisitions and mergers, they have become regional banking powerhouses and the envy of the banking industry. Wherever these two institutions go, customers follow. In fact, the outstanding retail banking performance of these powerhouses pressures their peers and other institutions to change just to keep pace with the McBankers.

Cultural Imperatives

When it comes to creating and nurturing a sales culture in a retail banking, the leaders are clearly in the minority. Both executives and front office staff in the trenches can attest to the severe growing pains as their institutions shift from retail banking to *bank retailing*.

Nothing short of top-down organizational change that values sales and cross-selling will remake retail banking. A retail banker at a recent convention mused, "A considerable number of bankers look at the fragmented, misguided sales organization in their banks and conclude that sales could not be too important, for management continues to leave it like it is. In essence, if selling were more critical it would be better managed, more productive, and a lot more visible."

Many bankers take the same reactive approach to selling that they use in planning. They prefer to wait, or move ahead with caution, in small, measured steps. This standard operating procedure of many banks, from money center to de novo, will not set the world on fire. Nor will it significantly alter retail banking routines carved in stone.

Establishing a sales culture runs deep to the core of a financial organization. A sales culture impacts the attitudes, habits, and behaviors of the bank as an institution as well as every employee. Evolving a true sales culture in a bank takes time. One banker estimated it requires three to five years of *directed*, consistent, and coordinated effort. A memo or a meeting will not a culture make.

"Customerized" Banking

In order to maximize the sales and cross-selling effort, bankers must get to know customers—intimately. A hard-nosed assessment of the customer information file (CIF) system will probably uncover problem areas that bankers overlook or prefer to avoid. When customer information is scattered in multiple CIF databases, it is nearly impossible for the bank and the customer service representatives (CSRs) to get a complete picture. Put the pieces of the CIF puzzle together and you will understand the customers' total relationship with the bank.

Bankers know well that making customer *convenience* a priority is critical for long-term success. In a survey of senior retail banking executives, convenient and courteous service scored highest on the list of competitive priorities. Convenience is evident as bankers move to extend the banking day, move branches into supermarkets, and enhance the functions of and access to ATMs and other types of self-service automation.

Improving the bank's *communication* with customers is another prerequisite for retail banking in the 1990s. Communication includes every customer contact from monthly statements to interpersonal encounters to the overall branch environment and image the bank presents. The marriage of computers and telecommunication provides new opportunities such as 24-hour account information and teleservicing using automated voice response. Online credit bureau access and credit scoring models permit bankers to implement the 15-minute loan by phone—slick and speedy service for the bank's most cherished customers.

Communication means asking questions and listening to customers. Soliciting feedback from tellers in the trenches and platform service staff is another suggestion. One reason why bankers have trouble understanding customer needs and effectively meeting their expectations is because they fail to know them.

Customers appear on every page of this book, just as they are the cause of every transaction the bank takes or makes. Customers are the goal; every decision the bank makes, every technological investment, is to benefit or serve the customer—at a profit for the bank. Everything else is expendable.

Calculated Moves

The partner of cultural change in retail banking is technological change. Bankers have been swept up by the sea of change happening in technology. Some call it "the fourth wave" of computing. Others call it the "tidal wave of technology."

In terms of the banking industry, the progression has been from systems that excelled in capturing and accounting for transactions to product-centered systems, dedicated to such lines of business as lending or credit-card management, to customer-centered relational database information systems.

In the past, bank data-processing departments moved in fits and starts, patching, maintaining, and upgrading systems to keep pace. The next stage is information integration.

Connectivity, the linking of computer systems and information to achieve customer insights and information exchange is the bankers' battle of the modern age. Middle managers no longer worship at the altar of the bank's MIS department; the data center walls are crumbling; bank executives are demanding free access to information and seizing a role in new system developments.

Implementing *custom, flexible*, and *dynamic* solutions on crash schedules is also the mark of the forward-moving retail bank—solutions that are customized for customers and employees alike. Technology solutions can be both user-friendly and customer-responsive. Nothing less is acceptable.

Breakthrough advances in technology can actually ease the growing pains of change. Computers, and micros in particular, offer myriad advantages to aid and abet the selling process, as well as for mining and managing customer information. Advances in product development promise the creation of new products tailored for "micromarkets. "The phenomenon of 'private banking for the masses' is definitely possible using available technology," states a banker on the cutting edge.

Commitment: Top-Down, Inside-Out

Moving from the top down, the next stop is at senior level management. Management must be commited to quality service, products, and sales. Retail banking executives need to foster staff confidence, which means career planning, ongoing training, and, dare it be said, incentive compensation. The bank's employees cannot become service stars until they have internalized the bank's mission and see their own supervisors practicing their sermons.

NO SIMPLE ANSWERS

Walter B. Wriston, the ex-Citicorp chief, says, "Over the last few decades, we have had many theories of business management. We have moved from centralized control to decentralization, and in some cases back again; we have pursued excellence, studied theory Z, constructed matrices, and even learned to be one-minute managers. The fundamental fact remains that those businesses that survive may change their partners and use new information technology to understand their marketplace and serve their customers needs in a better, more cost-effective, way."

There is no magic in remaking the retail banking organization to recast its mission and image. Begin by sketching the overall strategy: goals, objectives, action plans, and tactics. Then evaluate the existing structure: operations, staffing, support systems and procedures, as well as the dominant business and banking trends.

But there are no simple answers to the soul-searching questions. No single path of success that can be emulated by all. What works for one institution can just as easily fail at another down the street. Within the same institution one can find hundreds of branches, each serving a different mix of customers and markets.

Before leaping to solutions or buying the next new technology, every banker needs to stop and ponder: What is the real nature of our business(es)? What should the nature of our business(es) become? What is the incentive for customers to save, borrow, and invest at our bank? How do we move or change from where we are to where and what and who we want to become? These are the strategic questions to be answered by *Retail Banking Technology*.

1
Relationship Banking for The 21ˢᵗ Century

"Relationship banking" is the buzz phrase by which retail bankers define their wildly diverse strategies. However, customers probably have a better relationship with their butcher or baker than they do with their banker. In fact, in numerous consumer surveys, banking scored second only to insurance as the industry perceived as *least* responsive to customers.

Relationships grow from understanding and satisfying needs. All customers above the poverty line have five fundamental financial needs, regardless of their age, income, or demographic characteristics. These basic needs are to pay, borrow, save, invest, and protect or insure. Upscale customers acquire the added needs to manage the tides of cash flow and tax liability.

Historically, bankers have focused their efforts to meet the needs to pay, borrow, and save; other financial entities—such as insurance companies, financial planners, and brokerage houses—have addressed the customers' other financial requirements. Beginning in the early 1970s and continuing to the present, nonbanks have risen to battle bankers by nibbling away at the market share for fundamental products and services. In fact, an *American Banker* survey reports that 48 percent of consumers already use one or more "bank-like" products offered by nonbanks such as Sears, Merrill Lynch, and American Express, to name a few of the market leaders.

9

Some nonbanks started as niche product specialists, such as Household Finance in consumer lending and Fidelity Investments of Boston in mutual funds. As these and other nonbanks prospered, they made inroads in other areas and captured bank customers' wallet share and the yolks of their nest eggs. Some banks and thrifts have responded by venturing into uncharted waters and developing new products or forging alliances with third parties (including Fidelity Investments) for mutual funds and other investment vehicles to augment CDs.

BANK ID

Heated competition in the marketplace has also blurred the identities of banks, thrifts, credit unions, and nonbanks. Customers are confused as to which provider(s) can best meet their needs. Changing business requirements and evolving customer needs rouse retail bankers to examine their present business thrust, organizational structure, product and service development and enhancements, long-term strategies, and technological underpinnings.

An Account Is Not a Relationship

A customer relationship with a bank cannot be measured by the number of products used or the size of account balances. Rather it is the *quality* and *depth* of the relationship measured by the types of products owned, trends in the account balances and usage, and other "telltale" signs of devoted patronage. Bank-customer relationships, like personal relationships, must be based on understanding, communication, and respect. Relationships develop and change over time. Customer-centered banking means not only responding to customers' needs but anticipating their needs at various points in their life cycles.

Technology is essential to track customers' financial habits, interests, and expectations and to design, develop, deliver, and support comprehensive, full-service, relationship banking.

The Tale of the Tape

The untapped potential of existing customers, those folks that enter the bank's branches daily, can be evaluated by "benchmarking" the bank against some industry statistics.

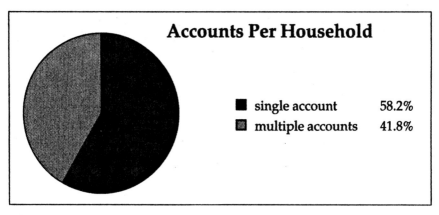

Figure 1–1. Single versus multiple account "relationships."

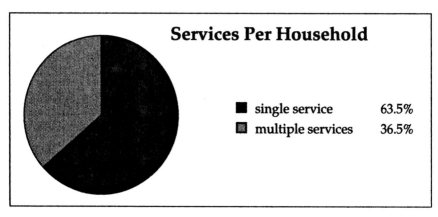

Figure 1–2. Single versus multiple service "relationships."

According to digested surveys from various industry sources, about 59 percent of American households have a "one-account relationship" with any single bank (see Figure 1–1). The percentages are higher for savings and loans (S&Ls) and thrifts, lower for credit unions. This estimate excludes "ATM card ownership" as a product. Bankers should be penalized for *not* putting an ATM card in every DDA-holder's hand.

This solitary relationship becomes more meaningful when the analysis is extended to *services* (see Figure 1–2), with service defined as multiple accounts within the same product line, such as multiple IRA accounts for a single household or a pocketful of CDs. Nearly two-thirds of U.S. households have just one service at their bank(s)—S&Ls score nearly 10 points higher. While there is no magic number of services a particular customer can and should use, a customer who uses three or more services with any one institution tends to stay for life (or at least until he or she moves). The average industrywide is 1.7 accounts per bank customer.

Customer "ownership" or usage patterns become more revealing when plotted by product and service lines, as shown in Figures 1–3 and 1–4. There may be no surprise to the pattern of household ownership of products at the "average" bank. Nearly half of the bank's customers have a checking account, nearly a quarter hold a bank credit card. Customers are already flocking to banks for mortgages as shuttered S&Ls and failing thrifts limit the choices. Banks originated more mortgages than thrifts and S&Ls for the first time in history in mid-1989.

The frequency of single-service usage is enlightening. Cross-selling opportunities abound and afford every banker the chance to bend the bars shown in Figure 1–4. Among the possible strategies:

- Cross-sell within credit clusters, such as an auto loan to responsible bank card charger.
- Cross-sell investments by tapping CD customers for IRAs or vice-versa.
- Cross-sell credit products to single-service depositors.
- Cross-sell CDs or investment vehicles to big balance savings account holders.

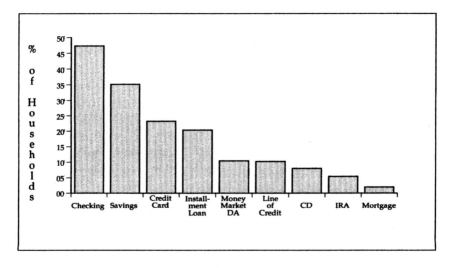

Figure 1–3. Customer household ownership of products.

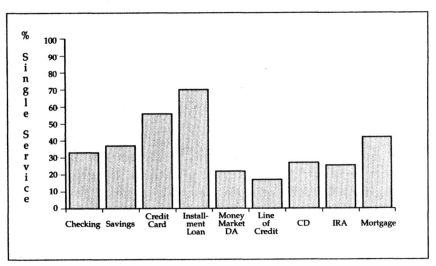

Figure 1–4. Frequency of single-service usage.

A few other industrywide facts are worth mentioning:

- Nearly two-thirds of all new accounts are opened by existing customers, and half of all new accounts are opened by customers who opened an account within the last year.
- Banks tend to have approximately one-third of their customers' total financial-related business.
- At the average bank, 20 percent of the customers account for 80 percent (or more) of the deposits; the top 1 percent accounts for 20 percent of the bank's deposits.

Industry averages are only averages, but they are better than the "guesstimate" assumptions that many retail bankers rely on. Bankers can benefit from some statistics-gathering and benchmarking. The exercise usually leads to some pleasant and alarming discoveries. If there is an industry fact it is this: Retail bankers cannot effectively move their institutions or change services and products (for the better) without a clear, objective picture of where they are starting from.

In reality, most households have *loose* relationships, or limited partnerships, with multiple banks. A credit card with one bank, a checking account at a branch of a bank that is near the job, perhaps a mortgage with a savings bank, and a car loan with yet some other bank. Young adults in particular shop around for the best value. They feel no particular bond with their bank. They spread their wealth and debt around.

What are the the differences between product-based banking and relationship-based banking? Relationship bankers target customer segments as opposed to taking a broad-based strategy. Value-added products and quality service distinguish relationship banking from the traditional pricing and standard product feature emphasis of the old school. Timeworn habits and "old-fashioned thinking" inhibits innovation. Every "traditional" bank product can be revitalized, enhanced, and made fresh and new, attracting attention and new customers.

New Definitions

There are four incarnations of any product, according to marketing master Theodore Levitt. When the classification scheme, as explained in Levitt's *The Marketing Imagination,* is applied to retail banking, it looks something like this.

At the *generic product* level is the "thing," the undifferentiated root from which all other products are derived. For bankers it is money, funds, currency, greenbacks, whatever you choose to call your basic commodity. It makes all banks, mortgage companies, credit unions, and financial providers equal. It is the entry point.

The next stage is the *expected product*. Traditional no-frills bank products are basic checking and savings accounts, CDs, and loans. The expected product also includes expected processes and services, such as the monthly checking/savings statement and the ability to deposit and withdraw funds in accordance with banking industry standards. Since their introduction in the 1960s and 1970s, ATM cards and bank credit cards have matured to qualify as expected products. Expected products define a bank but do not serve to differentiate one bank from another. Traditional bank automation and core processing systems, first developed in the 1960s, deliver and support expected products.

An *augmented product* is an expected product with something added. It offers a benefit or, in Levitt's words, "a bundle of benefits" for the customer. Integrated customer statements are an example of an augmented product and automated voice response for 24-hour customer teleservicing and account inquiries is an augmented service. Hybrid products—for example, "no penalty CDs" that combine features of CDs and money market accounts—also quality as augmented bank products. New technologies come into play at this level, as do staff training and retraining for high-quality, personal service. Incremental, tactical changes can add up to achieve strategic advantage; these measures attract and retain customers, and win customer loyalty.

At the top of the pyramid is the *potential product*. Some potential products are innovative twists on augmented products, while others are complex, granular, nearly unique bank products and services that break new boundaries. Potential products are the results of innovative thinking supported by technological breakthroughs. Image statements are an example.

CitiCorp has built a dynasty in the bankcard business—serving 22 million cardholders nationwide with over $23 billion in credit card outstandings as of 1990. Citi started constructing its plastic empire in the early 1980s, when interest rates were highest and bankcard losses were common. Among Citi's goals, when it had 3 million cardholders in 1981, was a 25 percent share of the U.S. credit card market. Through new cardholder promotions—many aimed at college students—and portfolio acquisitions, the number one bank in the land is well within striking distance. Citi has garnered a 15 percent market share and its bankcard receivables are three times the size of its closest rival Chase Manhattan. Citi's *CitiShopper* program takes the bankcard out of the customer's wallet and "motivates" use through incentives and special offers. *CitiShopper* is a great illustration of "bank retailing."

Critical mass is not the only way to position a retail bank product. In contrast to Citibank's national bankcard plan, Valley National Bank, a four-branch institution in Des Moines, Iowa, has a much more modest program—The College Savings Plan$_{sm}$—that transforms "traditional" money market accounts and CDs into long-term, goal-oriented financial planning programs. Each plan participant, parents and/or grandparents, receive periodic progress reports informing customers of the future value of present investments; adjustments or additional contributions to keep on track are suggested when appropriate. The progress reports, illustrated with graphs, are produced by using the bank's platform automation program.

Potential products are defined not by one attribute but by a cluster of value satisfactions that can be sustained over time. While many bankers aspire to the potential product, most fall far short of the goal. Potential products demand rigorous planning, expert follow-through, and the technological capability to launch, deliver, and support the product.

Bundles and Clusters

Bank product bundling is viewed by some as the latest craze in retail banking. But bundling, particularly among the institutions with $2+ billion assets, is no mere fad. Executives on the short list of "Bank Bundlers" (see Table 1–1) agree that selling a slew of bank services at the get-go has manifold benefits for all. Customers appreciate the convenience, consolidated information, and "privileges" offered by the bank. And a glance at the requirements reveals that these bankers are not giving anything away for free.

If the industry-average consumer checking balance is under $2,000, why do these banks set fee minimums at $2,500 to as much as 10 grand? The reason is simple—they use the bundle of goods to incent customer habits and behavior. Early feedback indicates that the strategy is paying off. Customers are signing up by the score.

Chemical Bank was an early leader in "relationship packaging"; it bundled products and services in a way that reflected customers' life stages, evolving needs, and growing net worth. *Student Plus*sm was created as the first step in a young consumer's developing bank relationship; *Select Banking*sm provides a combination of privileges and services, including an assigned personal banker, to the bank's "preferred" customers. When Chemical acquired Texas Commerce Bank, *ChemPlus*sm was adapted and renamed *OnePlus*sm for the lone-star state customers. In two years, approximately 110,000 *OnePlus*sm accounts were opened and attracted $3 billion in (much needed) deposits for the Texas bank.

Each bundled account plan is slightly different. Some are for the "50 Plus" preretirement crowd, while others are designed for the great middle market of American households—both urban and rural families. Norwest retail bankers believes in the family that saves together and offers free kiddie accounts; Security Pacific's bundled account has a "rather unique" sliding scale of credit card interest fees in addition to no annual fee.

Table 1–1. Bank Bundlers

Bundle & Bank	Accounts	Requirements	Customer Benefits
Blue Max Banc One Columbus, OH	Checking Savings Credit Card Money Market	$2,500 balance *or* $10 monthly fee	4.85% interest on checking No annual credit card fee Access to 500 ATMs for free debit card
Alpha Bank of America San Francisco, CA	Checking Credit Line Savings Money Market	$2,500 balance *or* $9 monthly fee	4% checking interest $300 overdraft protection Access to more than 1,500 ATMs for free
Senior Partners Barnett Banks Jacksonville, FL	Checking Savings Money Market	$2,500 money market balance *or* $11 monthly fee *or* $1,000 CD	4.25% interest on checking Free copying services Access to 570 ATMs for free
Citi-One CitiBank New York, NY	Checking Savings Credit Card Money Market	$5,000 average balance *or* $9.50 monthly fee	5.5% interest on checking Access to 1,100 ATMs; .$0.25 per withdrawal No annual credit card fee for first year
Financial *Connections* NationsBank Charlotte, NC	Checking Savings Credit Card Auto Loan	$1,000 balance *or* $10 monthly fee	No interest on checking Access to 600 ATMs for free *(Continued)*

Table 1–1   *(Continued)*

Bundle & Bank	Accounts	Requirements	Customer Benefits
Financial Connections *(Continued)* NationsBank Charlotte, NC			No fees on PLUS and Relay ATM networks No annual credit card fee for first year
Classic Norwest Bank Minneapolis, MN	Checking Savings Credit Card Money Market	$10,000 balance *or* $10 monthly fee	5.37% interest on checking Access to 720 ATMs for free No annual credit card fee for first year Free children's checking accounts
ValuAdded Security Pacific Bank San Francisco, CA	Checking Savings Credit Card	$1,000 balance *or* $10 monthly fee	4% interest on checking Access to 1,600 ATMs for free No annual credit card fee Lower credit card interest for multiple accounts
Interest Checking BayBanks Boston, MA	Checking Savings Money Market Debit Card	$5,000 average balance *or* $9.50 monthly fee	5.25% interest on checking Access to 750 ATMs for free Debit card buys gas at cash price

When bank products are grouped into a bushel or basket it makes cross-selling a lot easier than taking the traditional "linear" one-by-one sales approach. Pittsburgh-based Mellon Bank offers the SMART Account, which consists of 12 free or discounted bank products and services," explained vice president of retail project development Dick Gallerno. Mellon's SMART customers get free checking, no annual fee credit card, a free safe deposit box, ATM access privileges, overdraft protection and more. Fleet/Norstar's "Fleet One" or "Norstar One" multiaccount package comes with an ATM card, combined statement, and choices for clustered savings and deposit relationships. The platform representatives at these institutions also benefit by being able to cluster their sales or cross-sales in a sensible, predefined fashion. And with platform automation, the account opening and administrative details are streamlined and simplified.

The bundled account has another message for the customer—"Join our club!" People are joiners by nature, but club membership implies a "relationship" and usually some measure of "privileged status" in the association. It seems as if the American Express slogan, "Membership has its privileges," has not gone unheard by some retail bankers. Bankers should not hesitate to adapt or remold successful campaigns of nonbanks, or nonfinancial industries for that matter. After all, nonbanks have prospered by "borrowing" and imitating some of the best products and processes in retail banking.

A KEN FOR CUSTOMERS

The tendency to classify and categorize is human nature. It has not been the banker's nature until recently. Retail bankers are only just learning how to identify shared attributes of the local population and pinpoint customer traits. In *Leadership for Quality*, author J. M. Juran classifies customers into two groups—the *vital few*, each of whom is of great importance (which translates into the 1 percent of customers who account for 20 percent of the bank's profits), and the *useful many*, each of whom is of modest importance. Juran also stresses that any product or service will be deficient if knowledge of the customer is lacking.

Knowledge and understanding of customers, from the modest importance of the useful many, to the private and "preferred" banking opportunities with the vital few can be illustrated by examining key customer segments for retail banking success. One of the challenges is uncovering internal and external information sources about customers to formulate relationship banking plans and practices.

Baby Boomers Are Banking's Booming Market

They have been been known by many names. They were the flower children. They were yippies who became yuppies. The *Wall Street Journal* has called them "the unpredictable generation." They are 76 million baby boomers who were born between 1946 and 1964. Most are thirtysomething; the future of the country is in their hands and the future of retail banking is in their wallets.

To an extent, the financial needs and habits of baby boomers fit a predictable pattern, reminiscent of their parents. However, the sheer force of their numbers has enhanced their market potential. Bankers-who-know-best deploy technology to ride the baby boom wave of spending and saving. From sophisticated market research to Madison Avenue merchandising, from platform automation for expert cross-selling to convenient electronic banking services, bankers are capturing the attention and dollars of the "quality" young upscale earner. This generation of households need mortgage choices, ready credit to support fast-lane lifestyles, and savings plans for college-bound kids.

At the youthful end of the spectrum are baby boomers from 26 to 35 years old. Their real numbers peaked in 1989. They are the young and the restless. They postpone marriage and children, dress to impress, eat out frequently, and spend and acquire with a voracious appetite. When in doubt of their financial resources, they charge, as their older siblings charged throughout the 1980s. Retail bankers bear witness to the incredible rise in debt over the past decade, be it for first homes, fast cars, fine furniture, or fabulous vacations. In effect, bankers have fathered and financed the American Dream for the Young.

Baby Boomers at Home

MicroVISION, from Equifax Marketing Decision Systems, Inc., is a consumer targeting system that classifies every U.S. household into one of 50 market segments based on microgeographic, demographic, socioeconomic, and housing characteristics. With MicroVISION, bankers can target baby boomers residing in particular areas where residents share patterns of purchasing, financial behavior, and needs. Thirteen MicroVISION market segments reflect a strong baby boomer bias.

- **Lap of Luxury**: Very high-income urban families with teenage children. High installment account activity; high bankcard balances.
- **Established Wealth**: High-income professionals (ages 35–55) with school-age children. Medium-high installment account activity; very low retail accounts.
- **Mid-Life Success**: High-income dwellers 35–44 years old on the edge of cities. Two-income families in newer homes. Super-high installment account activity.
- **Prosperous Ethnic Mix**: Two-income urban families, high-income and education, average age is 40. Medium to high installment accounts.
- **Good Family Life**: Large families, white and white-collar in their 30s and 40s with high income and education. Live in new homes. Medium to high installment and bankcard balances.
- **Movers and Shakers**: Young to middle-age singles and couples who live on the urban fringes. Average credit activity; medium to high installment activity.
- **Building a Home Life**: Middle-age, high to middle-income families with many school-age children, suburban homeowners. Medium to high installment activity.
- **Successful Singles**: Ages 25–34, well-educated ethnic mix of predominantly urban renters. Very high bankcard and very high installment account activity.
- **Middle Years**: Middle income couples (35–44) many with families. Super high installment and bankcard account activity.
- **Country Home Families**: Rural homeowners in their late 30s and 40s with teens. Average income, education, and credit activity.

(Continued)

- **Bedrock America**: White, blue-collar suburban households with young children. Low installment account activity; high bank-card activity and balances.
- **Middle of the Road**: Middle-income families with school-age children. Many new account holders, super-high bankcard balances.
- **Living Off the Land**: Rural families with middle-low income. Very low credit activity.

Chapter 7 examines this phenomenon of micromarketing of financial products and services in detail.

Fortysomething Customers

The house-hungry 25- to 40-year-old segment peaked in 1991. From then on, the national housing market is expected to gradually decline regardless of what happens with mortgage interest rates or the economy. Mortgage bankers have already pared their staffs, preparing for the worst. At the same time the pendulum is swinging from spending to savings.

No other birthday causes the kind of gut-wrenching soul searching as the fortieth does. At this point baby boomers start to reevaluate their lives and take stock of their financial health and plans. Until 40, most people focus on short-term financial objectives, after this point comes "the long term." Evidence confirms that baby boomers do indeed change their financial habits. The national savings rate hit rock bottom at 3.2 percent of disposable income in 1987. However, by the end of the eighties, savings had edged up to 5.6 percent—more characteristic of the thrifty 1970s than the spendthrift 1980s. Maturing baby boomers are expected to account for more than half of the growth in savings over the next decade, which economists forecast in the range of 8 to 10 percent of disposable income.

The Nobel prize-winning economist Franco Modigliani of MIT terms the fortysomething shift a rite of passage in the "Life Cycle Theory of Consumer Behavior." Modigliani states that young adults are in the process of "household formation," so they tend to have low savings rates. As a group they are "net borrowers." Once they pass over to the other side of forty, they become "net savers."

Are retail bankers recognizing and capitalizing on the (financial) life changes that adults go through at age 40? Do they execute cross-selling efforts at this turning point of their customers' lives? Most bankers don't spot trends quickly, much less set trends. In terms of trends, bankers are viewed as the polyester kings of financial fashion.

Of bankers interviewed, not one does anything special when customers turn 40! Yet, both demographers and financial planners forecast a profound change when millions of adults hit the their personal 40 mark during the 1990s. The baby boom generation will be 35–54 when they hit the next millenium. They will be enjoying their peak income-earning years. If history repeats itself, baby boomers will be flocking to nonbanks for their long-term investment needs and interests. Mutual fund companies, insurance agencies, and the brokerage industry will benefit greatly from baby boomer mass withdrawals from banks.

Among the throngs of fortysomething baby boomers are today's preferred banking (those on the cusp of private banking) customers. These "preferred" banking candidates, among Juran's "vital few," are routinely ignored by many retail bankers. To an extent, sales officers who concentrate on preferred banking clients are the bank's farm team—the field where rookie financial planners gain experience and polish and hone their skills.

Retirement Planning

At the 40–54 life stage, financial advisors recommend savings equivalent to 3–6 months of living expenses in *very* liquid, money market-type, accounts—products that retail banks are famous for. Advisors also suggest increased life and disability insurance. American Express uses direct mail campaigns to solicit automatic, tax-deferred savings and investing from baby boomers nearing forty. Fidelity Investments offers a variety of annuity programs for long-term asset accumulation.

In a survey performed by the International Association for Financial Planning (IAFP), 59 percent of Americans over 40 viewed retirement planning as their top long-term financial goal, followed closely by saving for their children's education. Most Americans (52 percent) claim they "avoid risk" in investments. And this safety-first orientation is borne out by the investment vehicles most frequently used: savings accounts (84%), universal life insurance (39%), stocks (37%), money market funds (35%), and bank CDs (34%).

The other interesting finding in the survey was that, among the high-income group, only 7 percent chose bankers as the "type of professional most qualified to manage their financial affairs." However, 17 percent of the total public picked bankers. Some retail bankers may ask "why do we lose customers as time goes by?" But the more important question to ask is how can bankers build upon and strengthen each existing customer relationship at critical points in the life cycle?

Appealing to Youth

A new course for **Dollar Dry Dock Savings Bank,** headquartered in White Plains, New York, closely matched up with fortysomething customer financial needs and plans. The bank purposefully lured younger, affluent customers from both the cities and the suburbs.

In 1988, the average age of customers berthed at Dollar Dry Dock for 5 years or longer was 55 plus; only 5 percent of the existing customer base was under 30. The bank quickly turned its rudder

and shifted course to attract more youthful urban workers and suburban households. A year later, Dollar Dry Dock checked the profile
of new customers. The results: One out of every three new customers was under 40. Linda Lockart, former senior vice president at
Dollar Dry Dock, said, "The bank succeeded because Dollar Dry
Dock offered new levels of information, product selection, service,
and convenience."

Twenty-three offices were transformed from conventional branch
banks into multifunctional, financial centers with strong retailing design and shopper appeal. Among Dollar Dry Dock's strategic actions
was a one-stop shopping approach, consisting of a full range of
traditional deposit and credit products, plus such new products as
life insurance, tax-deferred annuities, brokerage services, and fixed-
income mutual funds. Other services offered in selected branches
included travel services, tax preparation, gold coins for investment,
and real estate brokerage.

Grey Power

The healthy aging of America, prosperous customers who live longer, is another prime opportunity for retail bankers. As of 1990, the 20
percent of the population over 50 accounted for 80 percent of retail
banking assets and more than 60 percent of bank deposits.

Society National Bank, based in Cleveland, is an institution that has managed rapid growth without losing sight of the customer or profitability. At the start of the 1980s, Society was a billion-dollar-asset state bank; 10 years later, after some well-selected acquisitions, Society started the 1990s as a $16 billion asset, three-state financial institution. Henry Meyer, vice chairman of Society National is well aware of the demographic reality of the midwest in general and northern Ohio in particular. "We are not experiencing population growth, and without the growing influx of younger families, the existing population grows older. To us, that is an opportunity because older people are savers and our 'Prime Advantage' group is where we raise deposits for Society," explained Meyer.

"The Prime Advantage program had such success that Society's 'merger partner,' TrustCorp, adopted the program under a license agreement," states Meyer, prior to the 1990 merger. The vice chairman continues, "With this knowledge of markets under control, we can turn to designing products."

In 1990, Marvin Mazie, president of Valley National Bank in Des Moines, Iowa, penned a personal letter inviting customers aged 50 and over to join "Our Gang." It is not a reunion with Spanky and Alfalfa, but a "special club" where membership includes free checking, one year's free safe deposit rental, travel opportunities, free bank-sponsored seminars, and more. More than 1,000 seniors joined in the first year.

Programs for seniors are not a new phenomenon, indeed, these age-based perks and programs can be traced back to the mid-1970s to such pioneering banks as the Santa Barbara National Bank in California. What is new are two developments: the minimum age keeps dropping from 60 plus to 50; and the retail banking systems of banks enable institutions to custom-package more products and services in a cost-effective, efficient manner.

When bankers learn about customers, they also start separating fact from assumptions. The growing greying population is not necessarily healthier; many are living longer *with* their illnesses thanks to medical care. Ex-Citicorp chairman Walter Wriston believes that bankers can profitably expand quality, nonbank services to their aged customers. Assistance with forms is one example cited by Wriston; filling out complicated medical forms (often printed in small type), preparing tax returns, and other clerical tasks are just as needed as travel arrangements. Bankers should note that H & R Block has built an empire in tax form assistance.

Continuity Banking

The best time to build a strong multifaceted relationship with any customer is at the first encounter. During the new-account opening the customer service representative (CSR) routinely gathers important information. The new-account opening is the best opportunity for cross-selling and bundled-account presentations.

One note of caution. Many banks and CSRs try to accomplish everything in the first 15-minute encounter. This scares the baby boomer (or any customer). A solid customer relationship is not built in a day. A relationship has a life. Banks need to employ a continuity approach to building and maintaining relationships with customers as they and their families grow.

Certain products become better choices for customer as their needs, circumstances, and rising incomes warrant. That is why bankers need to keep one eye on the information their customers provide on an individual transaction or product-usage basis, and the other eye on the masses. Marketing Customer Information Files (MCIFs), demographics, and customer profiling are important elements in the overall retail banking sales and service strategy.

THE QUEST TO PROVIDE QUALITY SERVICE

The phrase "Service quality in banking" provokes a strong response from customers who have been unwittingly cast in the tragedy of misplaced mortgage files, loan application typing boo-boos, and other bank blunders. Inferior and haphazard service is all too common.

Acres of forests have already been sacrificed in the cause of service quality—scores of books preach quality gospel. Instead of an extended discussion of service quality, let's review what bankers are actually doing and survey the contribution of experts, who present their cases quite eloquently.

Let's start with William H. Davidow and Bro Uttal's definition, contained in *Total Customer Service: The Ultimate Weapon* "Customer service is whatever enhances customer satisfaction. It is the difference between how a customer *expects* to be treated and how he or she *perceives* being treated. The elements of customer service are subtle, diverse, and sometimes surprising." Marketing master Ted Levitt adds, "Customer service means all features, actions, and information that augment the customers' ability to realize the potential value of a product or service as it is used."

Service is a dynamic process, and the criteria for acceptable or superior service are constantly shifting, depending on the customer. The customer actually defines quality service, not the bank. Bankers must put themselves in the position of the customer to best assess their quality strengths and weaknesses.

First Union Corporation, the superregional headquartered in Charlotte, North Carolina, has been quality-conscious for years. In 1983, the bank conducted a survey of their customers and discovered a four-part formula for service success: *speed, convenience, personal service,* and *simplicity* emerged as the key criteria.

Under the leadership of chairman and CEO Edward Crutchfield, First Union is a standout performer in the "high-tech, high-touch" retail banking. First Union bankers regularly "shop" their own branches, acting like customers to see if anything needs work or adjustment. Customer satisfaction is a guarantee: Any new customer who opens an account and is dissatisfied for any reason in the first six months with the bank can close the account and get all service charges reimbursed. No questions asked. And First Union employees are motivated to deliver quality, friendly service. In fact, branch managers are able to reward employees "on the spot" with bonuses for superior service.

What Have You *Not* Done for Me Lately?

"Customers usually don't know what they're not getting until they don't get it," warns Levitt. Customers will dwell on dissatisfaction, partly because many banks do a poor job of reminding customers of the value-added services they do receive. A little boasting goes along way. Keep customers informed.

Keep asking customers: "How are we doing?" Lack of communication is a root cause of customer malaise in retail banking. The reason why 15 to 20 percent of customers close their accounts with a bank every year is twofold: they are marketed away from the bank, or they switch because of dissatisfaction with products or services. Only five percent switch because they moved outside the bank's branching domain, although many retail bankers assume that is the primary reason.

Authors Davidow and Uttal hit another service bull's-eye in stating, "No bank can produce superior service, quality service, unless senior management is visibly, consistently, and at times irrationally committed to the customer. At many financial institutions, the customer gets lost in the bank bureaucracy. Policies, procedures, and processing take precedence over the customer. Sure, the customer is important. But is he or she treated like the "priority"? Not often.

At first glance, Baxter Credit Union, whose members are employees of Baxter, Inc., the world's largest health-care company, seems like a typical, small-sized (about $150 million assets) institution. However, upon closer examination, Baxter CU and president and CEO Rex Johnson are far from typical. Dynamic growth and expansion have marked Baxter since its creation—membership has grown from 14,000 to more than 55,000; a VISA card program started in 1986 garnered more than 20,000 accounts within three years, and the union averages 400 car loans and 35 home equity loans a month.

In November 1989, Johnson summoned Baxter's technology suppliers to the CU's Deerfield, Illinois headquarters for a meeting on quality. "We can't deliver quality services if our supplier is not part of our process. We demand that every supplier acts as our partner. Together we define the requirements, measure the outcomes, and evaluate and adjust to improve our performance," stated Johnson. His unwavering commitment to quality challenges all involved— management, staff, and suppliers—to deliver the highest possible level

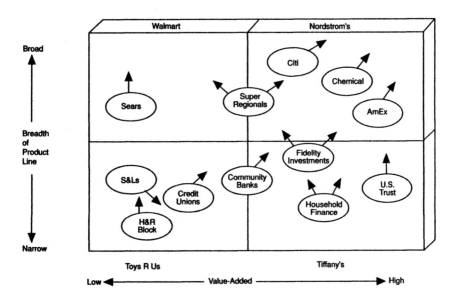

Figure 1–5. Perceived positions of financial industry providers.

of customer support. And in return, the automation vendors challenge Baxter with system enhancements that keep it moving ahead technologically.

Evidence seems to show that all financial institutions are gravitating toward quality and value-added services. Figure 1–5 is an updated view of service perception of retail banks and nonbanks. Nordstrom's department store is renowned for wide product selection and elite levels of service. WalMart is the most successful example of diverse product offerings at a low cost. At the other extreme, niche players in retailing can be plotted along the value-added axis, with Toys R Us at one end and the Tiffanys of the world at the other extreme. Where does your institution fall in the bank retailing paradigm? More importantly, in what direction is it moving?

Customers For Life

How do you retain valued customers? Addressing their financial needs and expectations are critically important tactics. This means broadening the bank's investment and savings product mix (and/or making strategic alliances with insurance, mutual funds, and brokerage companies). It also correlates with another tidbit of market research, which reveals that customers who use four or more products and/or services at a single institution tend to be lifetime customers.

The bonds that tie households with financial providers are personal and electronic. Retail banking delivery systems, integrated customer information, and dynamic ongoing service quality rest at the heart of every banking relationship. To be successful, bankers must review and affirm their commitment to personal, responsive, and comprehensive customer relationship development.

Bankers must also take the initiative to make relationship banking a meaningful lifetime partnership: a relationship that marks the seasons and changes in customers' financial lives from their spending and credit years to their middle age of savings through their retirement years of financial security. It's a lifetime relationship that should mellow and age like fine wine.

One final thought: *Keep the customer satisfied and you keep the customer.*

2

Information and Integration

While the value of bank systems and equipment can be calculated by its depreciated price tag, the value of vital, *integrated* customer information is immeasurably higher. Information that any bank creates, maintains, and manages may be its most *underappreciated asset*. This is the real end product of the bank's data center. Bank chief information officers (CIOs) need to be masters of information resource management rather than chief code mechanics.

Information is Power. Responsibility for the care and maintenance of the bank's information technology and core-processing applications is surely one of the most pressing issues facing bank executives of institutions large and small. Information flows through the heart and brain of every bank. It is not the size or the age, or even the hardware/software brand of the core-processing system that matters, but rather the wisdom it bestows upon its disciples—the bank's decision-makers.

Data → Information → Intelligence

While advances in integrated banking systems and software enable bankers to develop and refine new products and services in minutes rather than months, product development labors in the dark when the targeted customer segment is vaguely described or unknown. At thousands of institutions, aging customer information files

(CIFs) contain an abundance of customer and transaction data but yield little information. Using computer-assisted software engineering (CASE) and other tools and techniques, bankers are revitalizing their CIFs to gain competitive advantages.

CUSTOMER INFORMATION RESOURCES

The acronym CIF will be used because it is the traditional term from the flat file days of database technology. However, a better descriptor is "customer information resources" or "customer information database." The CIF can be a rich, responsive database, an indispensable tool. Or it can be the dreaded data abyss—a wasteland of useless customer misinformation.

The CIFs at most retail banks lie somewhere in the middle of this spectrum. Although database software technology has made significant strides in the past decade, CIFs at many banks suffer from the sins of past neglect, and this hampers relationship banking and realization of strategic retail banking plans and goals. Among the key goals for any bank's future success are

- A meaningful understanding of *profitable* customer relationships
- Eliminating redundant and inefficient operations in the quest for cost controls and noninterest expense reduction
- Building profitable, value-added core banking products and services
- Forging *team* management of information technologies and strategic customer information resources

It is amazing how many of these goals make their crossroads in the CIF. Retail banks that have lost control of their CIF or institutions that have failed to effectively integrate multiple CIFs are at a serious disadvantage.

Bankers with solid CIFs are in control of their destiny and are in a position to seek control of other banks' customers. These bankers demonstrate how a smart CIF can be employed to pinpoint quality selling and cross-selling opportunities. These bankers target customer segments and get their message across to prospects using database marketing techniques common in other retail businesses.

Many traditional CIFs are nothing more than transaction storehouses, dumps for data. In the 1970s and 1980s, as banks expanded their operations into credit cards and other businesses, they created offspring databases. Over the years these clone databases proceeded to multiply like rabbits running wild. There are paths out of the rabbit hole, but you need a plan, a system solution, and the commitment of a dedicated team to a better way.

Dirty, Doubtful Data

In a recent industry survey, where participants included commercial banks in the $1.5 billion to $30 billion-plus range, the five most common problems in retail bank CIFs were as follows:

- Poor quality control
- Incomplete product linkage
- Inadequate customer relationship view
- An inability to identify target customer segments
- Virtually no means to perform profitability analysis

Indiana National Bank, headquartered in Indianapolis, participated in the survey. According to a bank spokesperson, "Indiana National has a good handle on quality control. The bank has built in more edits to prevent gross errors and full-time employees do quality checks on maintenance and file changes performed in the branches." Keen attention to quality is the status quo. The "homegrown" CIF, which was first constructed in 1975, handles more than 2 million Hoosier retail and commercial customers' accounts.

However, at many banks there are too many CIFs with too little quality control. Errors are perpetuated and replicated in different databases in the system until the CIF becomes an unwanted orphan. Dirty data can often be recognized on sight. It's the same customer with multiple customer records due to misspellings, missed spacings, and name, address, and social security number miscues. The same person—John N. Doe—can exist under John Doe, J. N. Doe, and John Doe, Jr. The solution: periodically running the CIF through the scrub and match cycle.

More than 700 financial institutions have called upon Innovative Systems, Inc. (ISI) for CIF cleanup on a service basis. ISI's BANK-MATCH links suspected and actual duplicate personal customer records, while CORPMATCH integrates company files of the same firm. Other automated options for the laundering of customer information databases are available from such companies as Harte-Hanks

Data Technologies, which offers CIFer for name and address scrubbing and matching.

It is no surprise that incomplete product linkage is problematic at many banks because CIFs are separate, unequal, and uncommunicative. CIF integration can be a monumental task that frightens (otherwise stouthearted) managers from merging doppelganger databases. Conversion to a new core CIF system is often the best solution, but the costs and business disruption that comes with the decision makes bank CEOs mighty anxious.

Another shortcoming of aging CIFs is that they fail to allow for alternate search methods. In fact, some bank staffs view their CIF as downright unfriendly. Users need instant, multiple online access by either customer name, account number, or TIN (tax identification number). This not only improves the quality and usefulness of customer data but it improves customer service.

A sloppy CIF makes a mess in other areas as well. In platform automation, new account opening is a horror when the CIF is garbage-strewn. Some retail banks have become complacent with the sorry state of their CIF, while others busily work to improve database accuracy, flexibility, and integration.

Who Goes There?

Most CIFs provide a snapshot view of a customer's *account* relationships, defined by the account(s) held as well as current balance, recent transactions, and other account details. The typical CIF lacks both a historical perspective and the ability to perform horizontal, or customer segment, profiles. As a result, retail bank executives cannot use their flat-file CIF to answer a multidimensional question such as, "What high net worth customers, by branch, opened a high dollar amount CD in the last 9 months, who do not hold money market checking accounts?"

Data entered into CIFs is sufficient to service accounts or follow a trail of transactions but not to understand customers habits, needs, and expectations. This shortcoming of CIFs becomes painfully evident in private banking services. Very few bank CIFs have integrated their trust and core account CIFs in an area where relationship management is essential. CSRs at most institutions cannot tell that a low-balance checking account customer also happens to have a six-figure trust account with the bank. Furthermore, customer data on doctors, lawyers, and other professionals are often scattered in separate retail and commercial or small-business account CIFs.

When business units within the bank act like independent fiefdoms, guarding their own account domain, the prospect of a unified CIF is near impossible to achieve. This is one reason why mortgage-lending CIFs are administered separately throughout the industry.

Another integration barrier is clearly marked along asset/liability boundary lines. According to an industry analyst, "In the beginning, banks focused on liabilities and automated those functions and responsibilities. Later, they began to pay more attention to the asset side of the balance sheet." Any artificial boundaries, be they departmental or along asset/liability lines, are counterproductive in assessing the quality, depth, and value of customer relationships.

Frank Sanchez, executive vice president of Sanchez Computer Associates (SCA) speaks persuasively about the need of banks to view "customer relationships that can be customized individually." These are relationships that are "database-driven," yet defined by account ownership and activity. "At the same time, there is a need for the CIF to support decision-making in different departments," continues Sanchez. SCA puts its integrated banking system, called PROFILE, where it's definition is—on the Customer (see Figure 2–1).

PROFILE produces customized reports on demand, responds to online queries, and answers "what if" modeling questions. The system enables bankers to create new products, modify existing products, and build bundled retail banking offerings without drawing on MIS resources. The totally integrated CIF/Relationship Banking central database provides both customer profitability and product profitability insights. System modules can be purchased separately or as a complete package.

In 1988 the Bank of Bermuda switched to the DEC VAX-based PROFILE with the goal of converting and integrating 85,000 name and address records into a global CIF for its retail, wholesale, and trust banking customers. The system has tightly integrated the bank's front and back office operations, and easily generates combined statements—one of the benchmarks of a true relationship banking system. An up-to-the-moment, comprehensive customer profile, including trust, is also available on every CSR's desktop workstation. Sanchez adds, "A bank's CIF also should be flexible to accommodate fluid customer relationships that change over time."

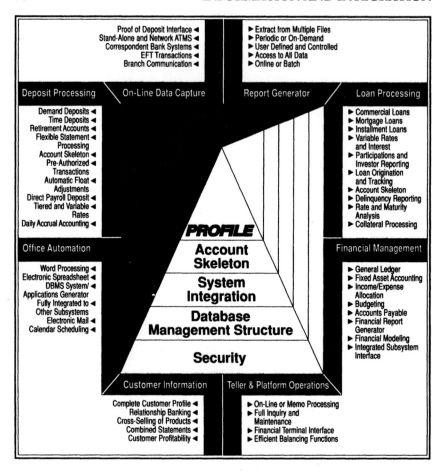

Figure 2–1. The PROFILE core banking system from Sanchez Computer Associates.

Wedding Rings and Other Things

Another component of customer relationships is the relationship between or among customers. *Householding* is a necessary step on the road to upgrading and integrating CIFs. Householding means recognizing the "familial" relations, those husband-wife customers who live under the same roof; it also should encompass home-based businesses for cross-selling and cross-marketing.

Some of the benefits are obvious, such as the immediate savings in postage by eliminating duplicate mailings to the same customer address. Linking accounts into households is invaluable for market research, planning, and promotional campaigns because it is the household that is really the decision-making unit for financial services.

Norwest Corporation, based in Minneapolis, Minnesota, is one of the champion regional banks. At the start of the 1990s it operated more than 250 branches in eight states, serves 2.7 million customers, and weighs in at more than $30 billion in assets. "Norwest's home-grown CIF was first developed in 1975," recalls a bank spokesperson. "Redundant databases handled householding, trust, brokerage, corporate account profitability, and other applications." The new Norwest CIF eliminated redundant databases and vastly improved customer file integrity. Combined customer statements, notifications, and bank marketing applications all run off the new core CIF.

Can a core CIF serve as an information-gathering, processing, management tool and as a strategic marketing database? According to an executive at ISI, "CIFs and marketing CIFs (MCIFs) are essentially incompatible." Most bankers adhere to the administrative database view of CIFs and believe marketing information and profitability analysis are best handled by dedicated systems.

A senior manager at KPMG Peat Marwick concurs: "The bank's customer information file (CIF) is the core of a marketing MIS. But it is uniquely different." In an ideal bank, the marketing CIF, or MCIF, links all the real and potential customer relationship components. MCIF systems can be utilized for the entire retail banking group as well as customized for private and professional banking divisions. Marketing CIFs and other resources for retail bank marketing are the focus of Chapter 7.

If there is a banking Tao of CIF, it is probably this eightfold path:

1. CEO and senior executive commitment and support to purifying the CIF and nurturing its ongoing quality and value
2. Identifying key users and prioritizing their needs
3. Integrating application CIFs into a central core system
4. Striking a harmonious balance between user friendliness and functionality
5. Clearly communicating CIF policies, procedures, and standards of quality
6. Establishing ongoing training of new users and, when necessary, retraining experienced users
7. Believing that the customer is the reason why the bank exists and that customer relationships are why the bank prospers
8. Ensuring that future customer relationships and business opportunities can build upon CIF foundations

The goal is integration of customer data into one, wholly comprehensive, core database—a treasure chest of information and intelligence to swiftly exploit retail banking opportunities when and where they appear.

CARE AND MAINTENANCE OF
INFORMATION SYSTEMS

Retail bankers know the symptoms: minor, annoying memory lapses, frequent errors, the gradual deterioration of faculties; then there are the aches and pains caused by clogged arteries; obstinate and inflexible behavior often signals the onset of more serious, debilitating ailments, and possibly a total breakdown. This is the sad but true tale of an aging core banking system.

The burden of caring for an old data center weighs heavily upon bank CEOs and CIOs, and it effects the performance of all—from senior executives to branch managers to the front office staff who deal with customers face-to-face.

George DiNardo, who spent 20 years building and rebuilding application systems as executive vice president of information management and research at Pittsburgh-based Mellon Bank speaks for thousands of chief information officers when he swears, "I never want to build a demand deposit accounting (DDA) system again." DDA is only one of Mellon's 185 application systems. However, as the 1990s progress, bank CIOs must question their long-held positions and biases. As competition increases and the pace of technological change quickens, DiNardo and his colleagues find themselves and systems vulnerable. If there is a moral to this story, it is probably "Never say never again."

CIOs at large and medium-sized financial institutions wrestle every day with maintenance of homegrown systems. Nearly half of the nation's largest banks rely on homegrown systems for their bread and butter DDA processing. However, programmer productivity at many of the big banks is poor and getting worse.

Industrywide estimates reveal that banks spent 80 percent of their technology budget on system maintenance. New projects and new product development all compete for a piece of the remaining resource pie, which is getting smaller. Add to this picture the growing backlogs of software recoding and repairs and the seriousness of the situation becomes shockingly apparent.

Those complex, convoluted COBOL programs that run many retail bank's key applications are written in a style that only the original programmer can understand and only Rube Goldberg could love. Homegrown becomes "homegroan" when fatal errors emerge as programs are modestly modified after years of relatively dependable service.

The situation not only plagues homegrown systems but also commercial software no longer covered under maintenance and upgrade agreements. The classical integrated banking systems were based on 1970s software technology. Over the last decade, legions of eager, well-intentioned bank programmers have patched, updated, and revised these masterpieces. Some changes have been for the better, others have been fiascos that have to be undone before the bank could restore processing order.

Robert E. Parks, president of Computrol, Inc. a supplier of core banking systems, elaborates on the "people problem." "In surveys that we performed of about 100 clients, development of an integrated banking system can require 1000 programmers and 2 million lines of code," explains Parks. The industry is short on programmer talent for such massive projects. Indeed, finding talented programmers to maintain systems in use is a battle that many banks and CIOs are fighting—and losing.

Prescriptions for Change

Daniel J. Sullivan, director of sales and customer support at Language Technology states "Bank MIS departments are under stress from four major forces—user demands, cost controls, technological advances, and software maintenance and management." Sullivan recommends software improvement to revitalize aging core banking systems as well as to design and implement new applications.

Software improvement is not like a fad diet, it is not an instant solution. As with any serious diet, it means changing the nutritional content of what goes into the system: changing not only the character and content of the software but the habits and work-styles of both the bank's programmers and end users.

"*Re-engineering* is one process to recover and preserve the asset value of a system by extending its useful life," explains Sullivan. In other words, re-engineering changes the underlying technology of the system without affecting the data or the program's overall functions.

CASE Converts

Reverse engineering, a subset of re-engineering, is a technique that involves going back to the specification level, tracing the origins of the application and its error sources. Bank programmers have performed this ritual manually for 20 or more years. The difference is that today there are tool kits and programmer workbenches that automate parts of the process. An all-in-one reverse engineering tool does not exist, but the advances in CASE technology seem to indicate that by 1993, it will.

Currently, CASE tools can only be used for new application development. A survey conducted by Performance Resources revealed that the most significant benefit of CASE technology is that system maintenance is less time-consuming and less labor-intensive. Researchers also found that organizations employing CASE had to overcome resistance from veteran programmers.

Is this a situation where you can't teach old COBOL codgers new coding tricks? Not really. Experienced bank programmers have not led the stampede to CASE because these software tools and packages do not cover their primary information system tasks, namely, *maintenance, enhancements,* and *migration* of existing application systems to new software/hardware platforms. Furthermore, there is a lack of agreement on industrywide standards.

Back in 1989, the *American Banker* reported that only ten percent of banks with deposits of more than $250 million were evaluating or planning system development using CASE technology. Among the banks that have pioneered CASE there are a few notable success stories.

A Case Study at Huntington National Bank

After evaluating all the possible alternatives—from off-the-shelf software to customizing a relational database management system—**Huntington Bancshares,** a $13 billion regional bank, decided to build a new CIF system from scratch. The bank choose to design and develop the new customer information resource using CASE technology from Texas Instruments. The landmark project was completed in June 1989.

At more than one million dollars in development costs, the project was a risky venture, but Huntington National bankers firmly believed the rewards were worth the risk. "We want to develop comprehensive, financial services relationships with our customers," states a bank spokesperson. And since the system combines information from several relational databases it allows Huntington's "personal bankers" at the platform to get an integrated picture of all financial relationships with each customer.

The bank also used CASE tools to plan, design, and develop new On-Line Banking Systems. Introduced in the fall of 1989, the software supports multiple applications for back-office efficiency and delivers real-time, front-office information access.

As of mid-1990, Huntington, based in Columbus, Ohio, was operating 253 offices in six states, serving more than a million retail customers.

In contrast to Huntington National, a stepwise approach to redesigning and recoding a core application system, such as CIF or DDA, may take five to ten years for the average bank MIS department. This may be the most economical solution to bring an aging system into the 21st century. But most retail bankers cannot afford to wait five or more years to rectify current customer information and core application problems.

Prepackaged Solutions

The Master Financial System (MFS) from Computrol offers advanced CASE technology and can be used to enhance a bank's existing operations. A veteran integrated banking software creator, Robert Parks, explains, "MFS can be 'wrapped around' a bank's existing applications systems to provide online relational search capabilities, standardized reporting, consistent screen formats across all applications, and user help screens. This technique, called *surround technology*, circumvents months or years required for new system implementation and also cuts down on training."

MFS illustrates human factors at play in new bank automation. Human factors technology makes for a more humane work conditions for programmers and end users alike. The underlying technology should be transparent to tellers and nonsystems executives. The system should interact with all users in plain English, not computer codes and programmer jargon, vestiges of the old days.

Computrol's MFS, which was first created in 1984, is a set of generic, reusable code modules that perform many of the necessary functions found in every financial application, such as posting, interest calculations, customer statements, file maintenance, and transaction warehousing. Computrol's research indicates that these functions represent 75–95 percent of the processing tasks in a bank application or new product development.

Subsequent program changes and modifications can be made online in hours. Since processing functions are shared within MFS, there is also greater standardization across multiple applications. Reduced maintenance time, operations cost control, and programmer productivity gains are real, measurable benefits of the system. Parks claims "MFS cuts maintenance costs by 80 percent."

"The system's modular architecture, well-designed approach to reusing code, and flexibility were reasons why Bank of Montreal selected MFS," says a vice president of system development. The system manages the bank's Registered Retirement Savings Plans, which are similar to IRAs in the United States. During the installation phase, MFS had to be modified for the Canadian laws and was taught to communicate in both English and French. Bilingual screens, selected by *user* preference, is mandated by law in Quebec province.

Marshall & Ilsley (M&I) Data Services is no stranger to bankers. M&I began data processing services for correspondent banks in 1964; 25 years later, M&I is providing data processing services to more than 400 banks in 32 states. Software Alliance, has exclusively marketed and licensed M&I's Integrated Banking System (IBS) since 1981. Forty-two of the largest banks in America, including 5 of the top ten banks, have selected and installed M&I applications for their mission-critical operations. Among big bank users are Chase Manhattan, Security Pacific, Bankers Trust, and Northern Trust. Expressed in other terms, 20 percent of all U.S. deposits are processed with M&I software.

During the 1980s, the M&I strategy was to link core banking application systems in integration layers with the goal of streamlining operational functions and enhancing system flexibility. M&I programmers are working on the third layer of integration—incorporating new product architectures and new technology for relationship management, information delivery, and emerging banking applications in a deregulated environment.

Distributed processing, improving system availability and data accessibility among applications, and reducing data redundancy are among the bank-requested solutions driving integrated software enhancements and upgrades.

M&I's Bank Control's database architecture enables bankers to side-step time-consuming application modifications and system administration. Each application "looks to" the core "Bank Control" module for processing parameters. MIS involvement in new product development or redefined products is minimal. In addition, the system features an extensive reporting system.

Will your core applications system support the bank's customer information needs and technology requirements in the 21st century? If not, you had better start *participating* in the planning process now. A common approach is to adopt a long-range perspective, and evaluate all the options—from phasing in new software technologies to rewriting essential applications to application systems conversion to facilities management or outsourcing.

MIS VS END USERS: FORGING A TRUCE IN THE TECHNOLOGY TUG-OF-WAR

You know you are out of place when you trespass into that frigid environment with blinking lights, whirling disks, and reams of paper shot from machine-gun printers. You have entered the data center, the information technology zone. For decades, a "systems mystique" has kept bank managers and end users at bay; even CEOs deferred to the wisdom of their DP Masters. Business unit managers learned to accept what they did not understand. Bankers bowed to the expertise of the DP Master and adjusted to "the system that imprisoned their information."

Times have changed.

End users—retail bankers—are storming the bastille. The unquestioned authority of the bank data center is crumbling like so many Berlin Walls. The questions to be addressed are

Who owns the bank's information?

Who owns access to that information?

Who should specify and build the systems that drive any retail bank's many lines of business?

Information Battleground

The grass roots revolution of retail bank executives and departmental users is a function of our times, an outgrowth of the technological evolution that marked the 1980s, particularly PC-based solutions. Bankers believe they now have enough knowledge to prescribe their own system, chart their own course, and control their business destiny. They believe the CIO or MIS director is out of touch, not necessarily a relic of an earlier age, but uninformed about the bank's business direction and strategic information needs. Bankers are through with the long waits for system refinements, through with being patient until a project can bubble up to the surface. They know their own priorities.

At financial institutions throughout the land, the basic information-processing policies and procedures of the last three decades are under attack. In this internal tug-of-war for power and control, the CEO must act before the bank and its customers suffer. The CEO has his own ropes to worry about. Often he feels drawn and quartered by pressures from the board of directors, customers, top executives, and shareholders.

While it is the CEO's job to ensure that managers work together effectively, he is less interested in the debates about technology or the ways to leverage information. He wants bottom-line results. In countless surveys, chief executives confess that the millions of dollars spent on technology fail to achieve the desired results of higher productivity, competitive advantages, or alignment with business goals. One point where CEOs and CIOs see eye-to-eye is their agreement that adequate return-on-investment measures to evaluate technology are lacking.

Meanwhile, bank MIS executives and the systems crew are trying to do (what they perceive as) their jobs. They try to support the bank's essential operations, and manage the transaction load. Retail bankers often refer to them as programmers, scientists, or engineers with limited appreciation of banking business reality. MIS people, policies, and procedures are not merely being questioned. Bank managers are demanding a complete redesign of the data management process, free and open access to information, and a fundamental change in the corporate culture of banking—the way people think, act, and interact.

Starting in the mid-1980s, business unit managers, department heads, and sector chiefs started smuggling PCs in the back door. They learned Lotus 1-2-3 and gradually acquired literacy in applications and computers. Now they feel they are ready to assume more control of vital information—specialized intelligence about corporate and consumer relationships for decision-making. They want reports in a format they can use. They want answers today, not next week or at the end of the month.

A key cause of MIS/bank manager confrontation is cost. Expense control is high on every CEO's list of priorities. The search for innovative ways to control the costs of product development, system maintenance, and end-user support inevitably leads to the back office. At any point in the next decade, between 10 and 15 percent of the nation's banks will be reorganizing, downsizing, or consolidating a merger involving back-office staff reductions or, at the least, realignment. If banks can move more responsibility for applications out to the business units, CEOs hope to become more efficient, competitive, and flexible.

One Banker's Lament

A deep throat at a big New York City-based bank, a frustrated veteran of MIS-end user strife, filed this report from the front lines. Banker X has served on both sides of the fence—in systems support and business unit management. He terms his bank's current condition as 'MIS mayhem.' "Nobody is in charge here, there is no such thing as strategic IT (information technology) coordination. Some business units run their own operations while others keep out of data processing altogether. Most departments fall somewhere in-between, with some involvement in applications development. So-called solutions grow out of necessity and work for a short time until the next crisis. Systems evolve or change willy-nilly."

To justify costs or "wasted resources" everybody tries to pick the pockets of the other guy's budget. When you are three or four levels down in the organization, you are fairly sure that no one at the top has any idea of what is really happening.

Solutions that should take six months take four years. People get disillusioned. They lose enthusiasm, or they just leave. End users think they want control of the system, but all they really want are reports they can use and understand on a day-to-day basis.

(Continued)

Technological developments move ahead in fits and starts without an overall plan. If you use the magic word 'open systems' you can get anything approved. As a result, the hodge-podge of hardware and software can't talk to each other or exchange information. We are building a Tower of TechnoBabble."

Another chronic problem, similar to customer information blind spots, is the lack of historical business unit financial data. Many bank data centers deliver year-to-date information, but getting a rolling 12-month recap is often a black hole or a tedious manual task. Retail bank executives need annualized and other historical performance data by region, or branch, or by-product(s). With such resources, decision-making is naturally improved.

A United Banks of America

To an outsider, the superregional known as **Banc One** seems to function as a loose confederation of community banks. Chairman John B. McCoy preserves the customer-focused values and home-town culture passed down through three generations that now extends to 52 banks acquired by Banc One over the past 20 years. During the decade of the 1980s, Banc One blossomed from a $2 billion state bank to a six-state, superbanking franchise with more than $40 billion assets.

Twenty-one consecutive years of rising earnings sets Banc One apart from nearly all other financial institutions. A careful blend of centralized information resources and decentralized decision-making is another distinguishing characteristic. Every bank, from the newly acquired to the original Bank One, belongs to one big online family for bank performance reporting.

The Management Information Control Systems (MICS) captures all financial information relative to bank performance on a monthly, year-to-date-, 12-month, and forecasted basis. Technology informs and educates; it also motivates. Every bank within the confederation is ranked according to performance figures and ratios. Peer analysis within the family is common.

Improved information access is the goal. Core banking and financial reporting systems should act as *delivery systems*—transportation vehicles—to get information to mangers in a user-friendly, automated fashion. As the banking staff and management become more computer-literate, MIS can provide the bridge between the bank managers who know what they need and why they need it, and the technologists who know how to make it happen.

Critical Roles and Compromises

Although many bank executives are entitled "Chief Information Officer," their corporate status and responsibilities fail to match the position. In actuality, they are treated as the data-processing manager, virtually ignored whenever strategic planning and business development is discussed. If MIS is to serve the needs of the bank of the 1990s, the critical role of the information technology czar must be acknowledged and expanded.

According to Michael E. Porter, professor at Harvard Business School and author of nine books, including *Competitive Strategy: Techniques for Analyzing Industries and Competitors*, "The critical role of the CIO is setting standards, ensuring compatibility, and creating interfaces." From Porter's purview, MIS acts as the facilitator, advisor, and coach, with the game plans coming from the business units. The CIO needs to look out to competitors, the market and customers, look around at departmental processes, and look up to advise the CEO on critical business mission alignment with systems. "This is not an easy task, and not common qualities among MIS executives," states Porter.

Part of the solution demands that business unit managers adopt MIS skills and procedures. Knee-jerk reactions to management demands or competitive pressures are a prescription for disaster. System integrity, data security, or information quality can suffer. When business units enlist the support of MIS for a departmental system solution—for lending, private banking, retail banking applications, or whatever—they stand a better chance of getting a system tailored to their needs. Business units also can find MIS as an invaluable resource for requirements analysis, proposal evaluation, and even contract negotiation.

Reconstruction

These are the times that try CEOs' souls and test the mettle of any retail bank's management group. Given the increased competition and highly volatile state of the banking and financial services industries, these are precisely the times when business units and MIS must work together effectively. The risks are too high to allow infighting or poor relations and low morale to fester.

One alternative to selecting a victor or letting the MIS/end-user battle rage, is to split the spoils—separate transaction processing (as well as voice/data communications, network management, mainframe maintenance) from strategic information processing. In a sense, transaction processing is a utility of the bank, a commodity, although a critically important one. Strategic processing includes all those activities closest to the customer, from marketing CIFs to profitability analysis, to the growing variety of electronic customer services.

A recent study, "Critical Issues of Information Management for 1990" by the Index Group, confirmed this trend in many businesses. Application development for practical day-to-day operations was being moved out to the business units; at the same time, management of technology and corporate databases was being "recentralized."

Complementing any structural changes there must be new or renewed personnel relationships—a healing of the wounds. Communication gaps between systems managers and business managers is the greatest single cause of failure in realizing the payoffs of automation. Perhaps yet another definition of *relationship banking* will emerge— partnerships among managers and staffs. People *networking* to get the job done. Team management with leadership support just may become the primary instrument of structural change for the bank of the 1990s.

Affirmed Alliances

Instead of bank managers attacking each other, bankers should attack their shared problems. At Norwest, the attack plan on technology takes place on three planes according to a senior executive: "There are the 'data processes' or areas where you can gain the efficiencies of machines versus the cost of labor; the product plane, where you seek to create new products and services; and the area of management information that can enable people to make better decisions and act quickly on that intelligence."

Tomorrow's retail bank information technology systems must mirror the bank itself; they must be highly flexible and superefficient at the same time. This requires a custom blend of centralized and decentralized resources. A dynamic blend of MIS and end-user strengths, talents, and insights.

The bank's information and systems are everyone's resource and responsibility. When bankers recognize this fact, not only can they move mountains of data, but they can mine the intelligence therein. Executives must deal with the emotional and psychological aspects of the MIS/end-user conflict as well as its economic and political dimensions. Where automation supports the best laid plans and schemes of ambitious and motivated performers, wondrous things occur. Controlled confrontation among professionals—those tugs-of-war—can be healthy, stimulating, and ultimately rewarding.

3

Teller System and
Service Imperatives

In the beginning was the word.

And for bankers, the word is transaction. The "average" bank, with more than a billion dollars in assets, "manufactures" about 140,000 transactions a day. People perform the bulk—nearly 79 percent—of every bank's daily transactions. Automated teller machines (ATMs) and other self service technologies handle the rest.

FACTS AND FIGURES

According to a 1988 survey, *Teller Performance*, conducted by the Bank Administration Institute, the average teller performs 20.6 transactions per hour. Top tellers can service a line of customers at a rate of one customer every in two minutes; tellering novices need five minutes per customer. Drive-up tellers transact faster (24 customers hourly) than their lobby counterparts (19.1 customers per hour).

Tellering is assembly-line work. The parts (customers) travel along the line to be worked on by a teller. However, while the traditional factory assembly-line worker performed a single task or specialized in a function, tellers are expected to perform a fairly wide variety of duties. And service is supposed to be fast, flawless, and smile-filled.

Evidence abounds that these smiling faces are not very happy with their lot in the bank. There are currently about 600,000 tellers in America, but millions have held the position at some point in their lives. Teller turnover is a scourge industrywide; roughly 3,000 tellers quit or are dismissed every week. A bank executive, based in New York City, admitted that teller turnover was one of the bank's most serious problems: "Teller turnover peaked at 97 percent in 1988; since then we have managed to cut that figure down to 48 percent." The industry average hovered at about 27 percent at the end of 1990.

In the coming years, bankers will face a severe labor crunch as they attempt to recruit fresh faces for their teller stations. One widely practiced tactic is to employ part-time and/or "floating" tellers, who travel like gypsies from window to window or branch to branch. And perhaps it is no surprise that banks are competing with McDonald's for labor. Both demand transaction-oriented, reactive, "fast food"-type job skills. Customers come in, are served, and leave as quickly as possible.

Cyborg Banking

In the Age of the Smart Machine author Shoshana Zuboff describes the dehumanizing dangers that automation can have on assembly-line workers. The factory approach involves "eliminating needless motion and effort, organizing tasks to require the least expenditure of will power or brain power, while quickening the pace. Skill demands

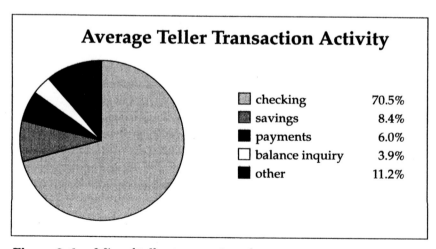

Figure 3–1.   Mix of teller transactions by account type.

are reduced. And machines assume responsibility just as they have assumed the skills, knowledge, and judgment for the tasks." In the quest to get more work from fewer tellers, some retail banks have "check cashing only" express lanes and employ automated cash and coin machines to save teller time in dispensing money.

The message in Figure 3–1 is that more than 88.8 percent of what tellers do can be done by a machine. And this fact has not bypassed bankers. The $17 billion-asset CoreStates Financial Corp., based in Philadelphia and owner/operator of the MAC ATM network, is one of a group of banks migrating to near-total self-service, using automation to decrease their dependency on humans. CoreState's "Branch of the Future" (see photo above) is an updated version of the "Automat" cafeteria applied to retail banking. It does not eliminate all the branch staff, but it uses a variety of customized NCR ATMs to educate and acclimate customers to doing things, including cashing checks, for themselves.

In effect, the customer becomes a "worker" for the bank. In a do-it-yourself environment the customer is the supplier and the producer of the transaction. Self-service automation is the enabler in the process. The human teller knows what is happening around him or her. They are expendable, easily replaceable by modern bank technology. Is it any wonder why teller morale is so low and turnover so high?

Most bankers question whether the near no-teller approach can succeed. As Michael Bal, vice president of branch operations at Provident National Bank, part of the PNC bank holding company, states, "To the customer, the teller *is* the bank."

To remain competitive and offer quality customer services, Bal and his banker brethren are taking a long, hard look at new automated systems that promise to boost teller productivity. At the same time, PNC and other institutions are addressing teller grievances and modernizing the teller's role in retail banking to improve customer service and satisfaction. And there couldn't be a better time.

TELLER AUTOMATION RENAISSANCE

At many banks, automation at the teller station is a generation old. The low-tech tools for tellers at small banks are 10-key calculators, an ink pad, and a date stamp. Controller-based teller terminals, first introduced in the late 1970s, are still a common sight in medium- to mega-size financial institutions.

Teller automation is going through a technological renaissance. Some bank CEOs refuse to sign-off for new platform systems without having their teller systems "refreshed," or enhanced. Available options include full-featured PC-based teller systems, cash dispensers that never miscount, signature capture to verify each and every check casher, and other electronic and mechanical auxiliary devices. And believe it or not, some bankers even claim that automation can increase the selling effectiveness of tellers!

Lofty Goals

Although the teller's job is high-volume and somewhat narrow in scope (check cashing, deposits, and withdrawals account for 90 percent of the action), it is not as simple as cooking french fries, or plugging in a part on an assembly line. A quick scan of the financial industry uncovers wildly diverse pilot tests and strategies in teller automation.

Although the priorities may be in a different order at the bank down the street, most bankers tend to agree on these overriding goals for teller-based services:

- Expense control or containing the average costs per transaction across the bankwide network
- Adjusting staff allocation and providing customer conveniences by using a blend of self-service automation and more innovative deployment of human resources
- Boosting productivity without sacrificing quality, or providing the same or better service to *more* customers with the same number or *fewer* tellers
- Improving cash management and control
- Achieving operational efficiencies by streamlining transaction order entry and eliminating tellers' manual tasks and processing interruption

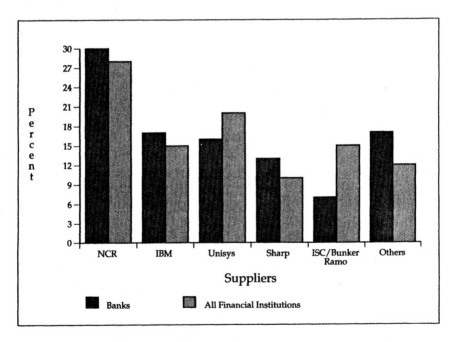

Figure 3–2.   Teller terminal census.

Likewise, similar system characteristics tend to surface in conversations with bankers who are currently shopping for teller technologies. They want systems with high reliability, flexibility, programmability, connectivity to other existing branch banking systems, and upgradablity. But what they really mean to say is that they want speed, efficiency, economy, and, let's not forget, swift, smooth, and trouble-free system implementation.

Hardware manufacturers dominated the first generation of terminal-based teller automation; aside from the merger of ISC and Bunker Ramo, the relative position of the top suppliers has not changed in the past five years (see Figure 3–2). But today's automation, wherever it is in the bank, is "software-driven." New PC-based solutions are springing forth from a variety of suppliers; it is important to do a thorough search before seizing any new system.

How Intelligent Need a System Be?

At many small institutions (and strapped-for-resources large banks), PC-based teller automation is still too pricey to cost-justify. Bankers are the first to concede that limited-function teller terminals are a quantum leap from the 10-key calculator. Although these systems are not as intelligent as PCs, one supplier calls them "smart-enough, and they connect with every host computer—IBM, NCR, Unisys, you name it."

For example, the compact teller terminal (shown at right) from Sharp Electronics has an alphanumeric keyboard, a five-inch screen, and built-in journal and validation printers; it was unveiled in 1986 and has been installed at hundreds of institutions, mostly community banks. One of the primary attractions, especially for small banks, is the cost—at $2,400 each, the per-teller cost is a fraction of a PC-based system. Another attraction is the ease of installation. A typical branch installation of four to six units can be done in a few hours. There is no need for any host computer modification of any kind.

At such institutions as the First National Bank of Omaha or Union Bank in Nanuet, New York, tellers use a Sharp terminal to accomplish their nitty-gritty tasks and duties. In addition to the electronic journal, there are programmable function keys for often-repeated tasks; cash in drawer warning, high and low check cashing limits, time management reports, and helpful instructions for both often-repeated and seldom-used customer transactions and inquiries. A new in-

terface enables the teller terminals to communicate with a branch PC-server connected to the bank's mainframe. This means that the teller system and a PC-based platform system not only can coexist but also can exchange and communicate valuable customer information.

The Berlin Wall of Branch Automation

A few years ago, there was a "Chinese Wall" between teller and platform automation, explained an executive in charge of systems and technology planning at ISC/Bunker Ramo. "Today its more like the Berlin Wall because barriers between teller and platform systems are crumbling. Technological advances—in software, hardware, and networking—are making it easier to deliver new functions and information to the teller."

At Los Angeles-based City National Bank, a $4.5 billion asset institution, an overhaul of the bank's 300 ISC/Bunker Ramo teller stations commenced in 1990. The bank's ALADDIN system, originally installed in 1982, was upgraded and enhanced to incorporate more customer information, product information, and new functions.

"Productivity tracking and reporting will help us to improve service and adjust our staffing to keep the lines moving during peak traffic periods," explained a vice president of product development at City National. "We use floating tellers, and now their balances follow them throughout their workday from terminal to terminal." Other key benefits are better cash controls, transaction prompts, and built-in instructions to assist inexperienced tellers. "The real benefit is a better level of customer service," concluded the banker.

Into the Valley of Automation Rode the 250

In 1963, **Valley Bancorporation** was a trio of Appleton, Wisconsin community banks with combined assets of $40 million. By 1990, Valley was a self-described "substantial, $3.3 billion asset, state bank" with 22 member affiliates operating in 60 Wisconsin communities.

In 1985, after exhaustive evaluation of branch automation systems on the market and input from 250 Valley bankers, the bank decided to create its own solution to integrate teller transaction processing, document preparation, and platform sales and product presentations in a single system. Today, Valley's PC-based, LAN-linked, Vboss branch automation system guides rookie tellers through any transaction simply by following step-by-step prompts; and programmable "speed" keys allow veterans to blaze through standard tellering tasks. And with Vboss's automated document preparation, cashier's checks, money orders, and bonds can be printed at the window, so tellers do not have to abandon a customer for a trip to the typewriter. This not only makes the teller's job easier and faster, but it assures that the bank's procedures are followed in a unified manner.

Since its debut in 1987, Vboss (which stands for Valley Bank Operations and Sales Software) has faithfully fulfilled its duties at Valley's 117 offices and is now used in more than 100 other banks. Valley's branch automation technology has also led to alliances with such industry leaders as Flserv, M&I Data Services, Newtrend, and BICS Bank Systems.

Teller Automation Shopping List

☐ Password security
☐ Online host database inquiry
☐ Concurrent host connections if necessary
☐ Full-function electronic calculator
☐ Complete electronic journal
☐ Bank-defined screens and screen fields
☐ Shared printer(s) and cash dispensing equipment
☐ Instant online help
☐ Instant cash-in, cash-out, and net cash at any time
☐ Display of teller totals by transaction type
☐ Transaction warehousing if branch server is unavailable
☐ Automated store and forward features for batch processing
☐ Document preparation for traveler's checks,
    cashier's checks, etc.
☐ Split-day feature
☐ On-screen void and alert codes with teller action required
☐ Ability to physically change workstation and have totals follow
☐ Compliance with Regulation CC
☐ Compliance with Bank Secrecy Act
☐ Speed keys for often-used transactions
☐ Page back on menu displays
☐ Supervisor access to teller totals and electronic journal
☐ Supervisor and teller override
☐ Balancing and proof screens
☐ Automatic printing at validation printer for specific functions
☐ Software changes and updates at the branch server level

Figure 3–3. Desirable automated teller features.

PC-based Teller Automation, using diskless PCs, can be linked in a local area network connected to a branch server. At first this appears reminiscent of branch controllers and dumb terminals, however, the features and functions that can be programmed far surpass the limits of terminal-based technology. Diskless PCs are attractive because they are inherently more secure; data security and data integrity are foremost in the minds of bank MIS executives. Among the scores of possible functions for teller automation, Figure 3–3 lists 25 of the most desirable features.

Technological capabilities pale when there is no corresponding strategy for their strategic use. Technology with inadequate training and retraining is another prescription for failure. Too many banks set aside too little time (two days on average) to train tellers in the use of new automation. Tellers deserve a better shake; they are a more valuable resource than bankers are willing to admit.

SERVICE PAR EXCELLENCE

Advantageous Opportunities

In 1986, executives from PNC Financial Corp.'s affiliate banks pondered many critical questions and issues regarding the superregional's retail banking delivery systems. "In the process," recalled vice president Bal, "we found that 90 percent of our customers only communicate or interact with our tellers. So we started looking at how we could provide tellers with the tools and training to provide the best customer service and take advantage of customer contact opportunities."

Coordinating self-service and teller services, and the use of PC-based networking, are the cornerstones of PNC's plan—the "Retail Sales System." According to Bal, "There is no dividing line between sales and service; 'quality service sells.' Instilling a sales culture means establishing acceptable levels of service and making those a constant not only across all member banks or branches, but in each and every customer encounter." However, the lofty sentiments of bank executives need to be embraced by the minions—the proof of the plan is at the platform and teller stations.

Perhaps that is why PNC has a ten-year plan, with ongoing evaluations and refinements scheduled all along the way. As it proceeded in the branch automation project, the bank explored innovative opportunities of PC-based technology. "Having the same software running on IBM PS/2s at both the teller and platform locations gave us a lot of flexibility. If the business case requires it, we can even merge platform and teller," explained Bal. As an example, he points to a "senior citizen" branch with no tellers—all functions are handled personally by platform representatives.

"Another factor we discovered," continued Bal, "was that 20 percent of the tellers' time was spent doing noncustomer functions. We set out to eliminate these functions, and if we can't eliminate them, then let's automate them." Bal selected and spearheaded the implementation of a full-featured, PS/2-based teller system using Broadway and Seymour's MAXIM software. System installation was completed in early 1991.

In a recently published Bank Administration Institute survey, entitled *Teller Management*, tellers' sales abilities ranked dead last among factors of importance in teller performance. However, PNC's Bal intends to buck the common thinking. Bal knows "service sells," although he and PNC's branch managers realize the ongoing need to nurture tellers' sales enthusiasm while preserving superior customer service.

"Sales is not not having tellers do full-blown product presentations," in Bal's mind, "rather its a quick information exchange, capitalizing on sales opportunities. For example, with our system, the teller can quickly answer a customer's question about CD interest rates or auto loans, or the system can give the teller a message that the customer has been pre-approved for a credit card, and the teller can refer the customer to a platform sales representative. There are lots of sales opportunities. On the other hand, the system can block out messages during high-traffic or peak periods so there are no distractions, just swift, accurate, friendly service. You can always ask a question the next time the customer comes in."

Information is a valuable by-product of customer transactions. Reports, productivity statistics, and other system feedback lets you know your products and services are where you want them to be. Armed with information, a bank can measure the effectiveness of its tellers and branch services and better evaluate other options, such as signature verification and cash/coin dispensing equipment.

Changing Routines

Customer identification at many banks means trotting over to a signature card file or to microfiche reader. In the past, many bankers planned to incorporate signature capture into a new branch automation system, but as they got closer to contract or implementation, electronic signature verification disappeared.

The reason for the change in heart among bankers is partly a change in technology. Signature display requires a graphics-capable terminal; the older, dumb teller terminals and early (circa 1983) PCs were not suited to the task. Banks that have already placed signature verification in the back office can now more easily bring it out to front-office tellers.

It takes three to as much as five minutes for a teller to check a signature on microfiche at some banks, and that means leaving the customer. City National is one of many institutions that has added signature verification to the bank's teller terminals.

Pin pads and magnetic stripe ATM card readers are alternatives to verify the identity of a customer, but "so is asking for a driver's license," said one banker. Signature verification is certainly easier to cost-justify if the bank is already using a host-based system in the back office and signatures are already captured are stored electronically on the bank's host computer.

Not Just Fast Cash

Minneapolis-based Twin City Federal Savings Bank installed its first currency-dispensing device in 1987. According to an assistant vice president at Twin Cities Federal, "Our experience with Cash Dispatch (a system from Inter Innovation LeFebure) has been excellent; it is phenomenally reliable and the tellers love it." The banker confirmed that automated cash dispensers "increase teller productivity by about 50 percent." The typical check-cashing transaction can be completed in 35 seconds at Twin City Federal's 12 high-traffic, drive-up locations, where two tellers share each machine.

The device stores cash in cassettes that can dispense up to 15 bills per second, either according to the customer's wishes or in the auto-mix mode (see photo at right). Eliminating the need to count outgoing cash saves one minute per transaction. "Not counting money was a real culture shock for the tellers," recalled the banker. The unit also provides a complete record of every transaction that makes end-of-day balancing a breeze.

Inter Innovation is also inventing an electromechanical gizmo named "Teller Cash Input," which counts bills, confirms the amount, and even checks for counterfeits. Already in use in Europe, the device is being secretly tested at two U.S. institutions.

Part of some banks' teller game plan is hands-off cash management. Between the Teller Cash Input device and Cash Dispatch sits SAL—the Sorter and Loader—a machine where bills are separated and bundled by denomination into cassettes for use in a cash dispatch or ATM. By the way, substandard bills are automatically side-tracked for return to the nearest Federal Reserve Bank.

Cash dispensers are not for every teller. Customer traffic, particularly at drive-up locations, seems to be the determining factor. Some bankers observe that, if you are going to spend that much money to automate the transaction, you don't need a real teller—you can do it self-service style.

In addition to the self-service solutions at CoreStates Financial Corp., NCR Corp., which has roughly 25 percent of the teller automation market and is the market leader in ATMs, is testing a novel approach in bringing technology to bear on teller functions. According to NCR's industry director for branch automation, "NCR's Teller-Assisted Automation puts online ATMs, which can dispense cash and coin and give the customer a receipt of the transaction, in the teller lines. Three machines are monitored by a single teller. If someone needs assistance, the teller comes out from behind a window or partition to offer help." In addition, the machines do not require the use of ATM cards.

In 1990, Bank South of Atlanta began piloting NCR's Teller-Assisted Automation. Part of Bank South's plan calls for placing Teller-Assisted machines in supermarkets, where the bank typically has a three-person staff. A large percentage of supermarket teller transactions involve cashing of payroll checks drawn against Bank South. Other banks are experimenting with drive-up ATMs to augment tellers who service car-based customers. The end goal is to serve more customers with less staff in a cost-effective manner.

While a lobby or through-the-wall ATM costs in the $25,000 range, the "souped-up" NCR Teller-Assisted machines may cost up to three or more times that amount. Which is also four or more times the cost of a teller. With payback stretching over a more than five-year period, this may be a most pricey alternative to real people. An extended discussion of the enhanced value of ATMs continues in Chapter 5.

Teller Road Show

Chemical Bank is putting tellers out to pasture in the fields of corporations, hospitals, colleges, and hotels. As part of Chemical's "Bank at Work" program, a specially designed compact, mobile branch built by Inter Innovation LeFebure, rolls around New York City to reach employees at their workplace.

"Banking à la Carte$_{sm}$" was literally rolled out in January 1988. Each unit accommodates two tellers, and can be set up in a snap in the cafeteria, employee lounge, or in an empty office. In addition to payroll check cashing, a full complement of teller-delivered services— from credit card and loan payments to deposits and withdrawals, and funds transfers can be performed. On-site transactions actually take place offline, but are processed before the end of the banking day.

The program also includes installation and maintenance of private ATMs at the office and "preferred" bank product package for new Chemical customers. According to a Chemical Bank spokesperson, "The program brought in 7,000 new household relationships in 1989, but the number is probably understated because some employees prefer to open accounts at a regular brick and mortar branch." Experienced tellers-to-go receive special training in customer service orientation and operation of the cart teller system.

The Bank at Work program works on a number of different levels. It serves to strengthen Chemical's relationship with important corporate clients, and can be an effective countermove for companies considering the formation of a credit union.

More than 50 Big Apple companies participated in the program in 1989, and Chemical aimed to add another 20 in 1990, including companies in its Chemical Bank New Jersey and Texas Bank of Commerce branch territories. The bank also plans to franchise the bankwagon program to financial institutions in noncompetitive markets.

Banking à la Carte is a service mark of Chemical Bank.

Service with a Smile, a System, and a Strategy

Will high-tech teller-line technologies make the difference in the long run? "Teller automation is only one part of the retail sales system, said PNC's Bal. "You can't just think of the teller in isolation, you have to look at your overall retail delivery strategy."

Evolving technologies give bankers more options and "insurance" against premature obsolescence than ever before. Some banks can migrate from existing teller systems to industry-standard, open systems. And those bankers bringing technology to tellers for the first time can choose from a variety of systems that provide a clearer path for future enhancements and upgrades.

Another gut-level question that many bankers are afraid to ask is: How much automation is too much? What is the optimum mix of automated self-service and personal service? There are no simple, easy answers. And answers often differ when posed on a branch-to-branch basis.

In retail banking, superior customer service and convenience will differentiate the leaders from the laggards. Check cashing and all those other teller transactions are commodity services. The fact remains that bankers win customers with quality personal service. If automation is not "embraced" by the teller, it will alienate the teller. The fascination with speed, getting customers out the door as fast as possible, will lead to higher levels of automatic, "impersonal" service delivery—a most undesirable outcome. Bankers can expect to set new records of teller turnover in pursuit of this strategy as well.

Customers don't care about the features or functions of the teller's system or what goes on behind the screen. But when these technologies, hidden from the customer, enable tellers to be competent, professional, and confident in their job, it makes them happy. Could it be that personalized service with a smile is the most valuable dividend of bankers' investments in teller automation?

4

The Promise of Platform Automation

RISKS AND REWARDS

The interior of many retail banks remind customers of those grand, old theater lobbies. A fitting association, since so many comedies and tragedies are performed daily at banks. Customer service representatives (CSRs) are the Keystone Cops of banking—they have the best intentions but frequently look foolish to their audience because they lack the tools, training, and direction to be truly effective product sales and marketing professionals.

In the old days, as recent as last week at some financial institutions, CSRs were considered no better than "clerks," expected to perform routine administrative duties. From helping customers fill out new-account forms to placing reorders for checkbooks to handing out brochures and applications—the job demanded light skills and some typing. During the course of the workday, CSRs fielded calls from customers or the main office, OK'd checks, and made customer account file changes on-demand but usually offline. It was a simpler, gentler time in retail banking before the age of the sales culture. Cross-selling had not been invented yet.

All of a sudden the CSR has become the front-office power forward in the full court press on customers. They are expected to be friendly but aggressive sellers of bank products and services, swift but "responsive" in dealing with service requests, and "open" to take on chores in customer file maintenance formerly handled by the back-office staff. To a great extent, CSRs have been shanghaied into serving aboard the good ship platform automation.

A number of banks are high on CSRs and platform automation. Bankers believe technology is the means to boost product sales, make productivity soar, build market share, deliver tip-top customer services, and achieve an all-around flashy image as a high-tech innovator. Other desirable outcomes are better cost control, a firmer grasp on product and customer profitability, standardization of product features across multibank holding companies, and "seamless" integration of customer information. Certainly the rewards of platform automation are noble, but why do so many platform automation projects fail to hit their target objectives?

The answer: Platform automation is such a complex process of people and systems, timing and training, that there are countless opportunities for failure. The risks of implementing new branch automation systems are exceedingly high. Many bankers seem to ignore nearly *everything* except the equipment, software, and costs in the branch automation process. It is as if bankers believe they can take base metals and microelectronics and create golden opportunities and competitive advantages.

Critical Encounters

The new account opening event is the single, most important customer contact in a person's relationship with the bank. On one side of the desk, the customer's first impressions shape his or her response to all subsequent cross-selling encounters. From the bank's perspective, information gathered by the CSR shapes the bank's view of the customer and his or her worth. Any ongoing relationship is based to a great extent on the data gathered at this critical encounter. This event is comprised of two information elements—the transaction (product sold and amount) and the description of the new customer. With these data in hand, the bank starts building a profile of and a relationship with the customer.

Not surprisingly, the three primary attributes of platform automation match the range of job responsibilities of the CSR, which are as follows:

1. Service
2. Administration
3. Sales.

Automation is supposed to shuffle the time allocated for these three responsibilities, however—more time for sales, more streamlining and time-saving for administration and service. Advances in desktop presentation graphics, "what-if" financial analyses, and expert systems that do behind-the-screen product selection for cross-selling are among platform system features that are intended to help to boost revenues. At a keystroke, product knowledge is delivered in nanoseconds to the screen.

Bankers are slow to admit the many hidden agendas in automating the platform. Improved communications and customer-bank interaction is supposed to be a soft-payback of technology. Another hidden objective, at least hidden from the customer, is moving back-office functions on to the desks of front-office CSRs. Cost savings are achievable from eliminating operational redundancies.

Platform Star Performers

In retail banking, platform success hinges on people and the quality of service they provide to customers in face-to-face encounters. Platform personnel need to impress the audience with their ready responsiveness, sincere enthusiasm, and professionalism. They must demonstrate the ability to serve competently and with a personal, winning style. CSRs play the leading role in the retail banking show. See Table 4–1.

They need to know their lines and appear natural as they deliver the product information and "sell" the benefits of banking at your institution. CSRs need superlative interpersonal skills because they are required to ad lib and improvise in their daily dealings with customers. Another characteristic of the star CSR is "problem-solving skills." The best platform pros instill a feeling of trust and make customers glad they came to get something worked out. It may not be a cathartic experience, but a visit to the bank to solve a problem should not be a long wait on line to see an unhelpful scatterbrain either.

The best platform stars develop a natural rapport with customers; they make customers feel as if they have a relationship with the *person* at the bank, not just a relationship measured by the number of the bank's products they use. It goes without saying that customers are not computer hackers, they do not want a relationship with a machine that sits on the CSR's desktop. A banker's reminder: "Every CSR or salesperson in the bank has a particular style that works for them;

don't let a PC interfere in the process. The PC, or platform terminal, should stimulate conversation, not replace it."

Table 4-1. A CSR's Diary—Where Does the Week Go?

Activity		Percentage of Week
Services		
Responding to a new account opening		10
Maintenance of existing account		7
Solving problems (check approvals, balances, etc.)		7
Counseling customers on products/services		5
New loan applications and explanations		5
Explaining rates, fees, services charges		5
Answer questions		5
Reconciling statements		5
	Subtotal	49%
Administrative		
Gathering customer info for new account		10
Typing, filling out forms with customers		7
Learning about new products and services, etc		5
Scheduling dates, deadlines, work		5
Rate fee changes		3
	Subtotal	31%
Sales		
Presenting financial products services		5
Qualifying a customer for loan or product		3
Cross-selling other products (after first sale)		3
Determining product service needs		3
Follow-up activities with customers		3
	Subtotal	17%
Miscellaneous		3
	Total	**100%**

Product knowledge is a prime attribute by which CSRs are measured. Ten years ago the average bank offered 20 to 25 different consumer products and services; today it is not uncommon for a bank to have more than 200 different products and services. Given the increasing number and complexity of products at most banking institutions, CSRs must feel as if they are contestants on a *Jeopardy* game show. To an extent they know the answers, but they are not sure of, or fast enough with, the questions. Asking the right questions to assist the customer in making the right decisions is a distinguishing trait of the professional, sales-savvy CSR.

Bank South, the $5 billion-asset institution that caters to customers' financial needs in Georgia and the Florida panhandle, replaced dumb terminals on the platform with a PC-based automation system. According to Bank South's director of MIS, "the goals of the bank are to automate as much of the mechanics of account opening as possible to free the CSRs to cross-sell during the initial encounter. When a new account is opened, the system automatically places a checkbook order, produces a debit card, and prints all the forms the customer needs to sign." Another attraction of IBM PS/2s at the platform level was their "invisible" information gathering ability. Not only does the bank better understand what and where it is selling and cross-selling, they know *when* sales happen. This insight has paid off in terms of "assessing staff needs and rescheduling to handle peak activity times."

The ability to capture vital customer information and improve the interaction between customer and bank employee are worthwhile goals, eliminating, wherever possible, those paper-based administrative tasks that consume valuable customer contact time during the new-account opening process. Automating these tasks boosts productivity, and that (in theory) means more sales, more revenues, more profits.

Furthermore, platform automation can and should support platform personnel in servicing both prospective and current customers. Once again the ties that bind are *personal* and *electronic*.

Presentation Graphics

At many institutions, the director of retail banking is searching for intelligent PCs or workstations that provide more functionality and colorful graphics that can enliven product presentations and enlighten the customer. Color monitors and graphics software are frequently on the list when the director goes shopping for new platform technology; however, they often fail to make the final cut when the final decisions are made. Cost is one reason. Another cause for the demise of presentation color graphics is that it is perceived to require different or additional staff talents—skills that are not worth developing and refining. Other reasons include the fear that maintenance, updating, and reprogramming will become an unwieldy burden for the behind-the-scenes crew.

Industry surveys indicate that fewer than 10 percent of the top banks effectively use desktop presentation graphics in their platform operation. But more than 25 percent of bankers polled would like to add it at to the platform show after a new (or upgraded) system is firmly in place and running smoothly.

One bank that has effectively used graphics-enhanced product presentations is Puget Sound National Bank based in Tacoma, Washington. This institution, with $3 billion in assets and nearly 100 branches, enjoys a whopping 41 percent market share in its domain. According to a Puget Sound vice president, the bank implemented platform automation back in the early days—1984—using dumb terminals. The banker also offers two bits of sound advice: "Sell benefits, not features, of bank products and keep the product presentations simple."

High-impact color graphics, including graphs and charts, can dramatically point out the benefits of different savings and investment instruments from savings accounts to CDs and IRAs. They can also illustrate the options a customer has in making a loan, mortgage, or home equity borrowing decision. Branchbanker from the Ampersand Corporation of York, Pennsylvania, is now in its tenth revision. The menu-driven, PC-based platform system can be found in more than 300 banks. Using the Branchbanker *SellScreen*, a CSR can begin a color product presentation at the touch of a key. Multiple presentations for a single product as well as bilingual text are options that have been implemented by a number of banks. A special-effects utility allows text and graphics to be displayed, using TV-like dissolves and wipes.

Other branch automation systems allow bankers to develop screens for desktop presentations or "capture" graphics from such popular PC-based software as IBM Storyboard, Harvard Graphics, or other paint and draw programs. One supplier has introduced a "library of banking and financial graphics" to enable banks to create custom product presentations more quickly. Help screens are also available, at the touch of a key, to cue and guide the CSR.

At best, technology is a prop or a tool. When platform presentation graphics is misused, it can lead to some embarrassing moments for both the CSR and the customer. One of the pitfalls of platform graphics is "the cue card syndrome," where screens containing too much text are read by the CSR to each and every new customer. It reminds me of an experience that I (and, I'm sure, thousands of others) had when I opened a new checking account at a local bank. The CSR was a very pleasant older woman who proceeded to walk me through a flip-chart of check styles. "No I don't want the checks with pictures of furry little animals," I said. "I just want plain checks with my name and address." Undaunted, she flipped to the next page and continued, "Perhaps you would like the checks with scenes of outdoor sports?" And on and on. . . . The "one size fits all" tactic is old-style banking at its deadliest. Graphics display software that merely perpetuates boring, repetitious routines adds no value or personalization to the platform selling process.

A second pitfall of platform graphics presentations is the "animated cartoon/special effects infatuation." For some reason, certain banks feel as if new customers are looking for Nintendo-style presentations and razzle-dazzle entertainment. At a recent banker's convention, attendees watched a display of a shocking pink piggy bank that winks at the customer during the product presentation. The pig grows larger and larger on the screen as the value of the customer's savings increase. This may appear cute to some depositors, but pity the poor platform representative who must watch reruns of this show dozens of times a day.

The real value of desktop presentations is how they can personalize the CSR-customer encounter. Eye contact with the customer and touching the screen is an easy-to-learn and effective sales technique. Desktop presentations can employ an all-text outline approach to impart product information. In fact, a banker in charge of a recently installed platform automation system refused to entertain picture-based graphics. "The screens should be informational not cute," he said. "The four or five major benefits of a product appear on the first screen, subsequent screens support the benefits; fees and restrictions are shown later; a cross-sell slide or screen should be the last in every product presentation."

Record Keeping and Ticklers

Selling activities of the CSR during a customer encounter—date of visit, products reviewed, "what-if" scenarios, and time spent with the customer—can be automatically recorded and can be used for follow-up contact or when the customer returns.

Precustomized letters can also be automatically printed for follow-up. Platform automation can and should streamline account-opening procedure and document preparation to ensure that CSRs have more time to sell and cross-sell.

An industry consultant, acutely attuned to the needs of banks emphasizing interactive sales functions, explained, "CSRs need to profile the customer's needs in response to probing questions, such as how much would you like to invest? for how long? and how liquid does your investment need to be? In an ideal world, the platform automation system should review a matrix of the bank's offerings and suggest those that meet the customer's particular requirements."

The integration of customer information and access to product descriptions during the new-account opening process should not be sidestepped or jerry-rigged in new system implementation. In addition to text and graphics, the system should fully integrate account opening, graphic product information, and financial counseling. The customer should not have to wait while the CSR shifts between account setup, transaction processing, customer service, and sales.

Facts and Figures

Calculations are at the core of "what-if" financial counseling scenarios. Any platform system worth its salt, or silicon, should be able to perform "what-if" financial analysis on demand, using the customer's dollar deposit amount or loan requirement. The "what-if" modeling abilities of certain software in the hands of a skillful (and trained) CSR can enable a customer to compare and contrast your products with those of the bank down the street to show the flaws and follies of the competition.

The platform system should be a "coach" for the CSR, guiding him or her through the process in response to the customer's individual banking needs and interests. At the most basic level, the computer should prevent the CSR from making errors, such as opening a checking account for less than the minimum balance or allowing a customer to apply for a jumbo CD without a jumbo-enough amount. It should be easy to program the platform system with the acceptable ranges for each bank product. Eliminate faux pas and common mistakes of oversight and order entry.

Using financial modeling software at the platform, a CSR can show a customer the cost difference between an automobile lease or purchase, or a discounted student loan versus a second mortgage for funding an offspring's college education. Software-driven presentations of investment options and/or product assessment for consumer borrowing and mortgage loans can improve the "image of the bank" while it meets the customers' financial needs.

A senior vice president at Chemical Bank, emphasized the coaching value of the platform system. "Genesys, our sales systems, is remarkably helpful to our bankers in closing a sale; data about a customer's existing accounts is easily and quickly accessed. Product features are easily described and compared with each other," he continued, "as well as with competitors' products. It will become even more important as the product line becomes increasingly more complex and as we get more knowledgeable about matching product features with customer segments."

Wilmington Trust takes this "what-if" modeling one step further. "The bank's platform software has the power to provide customers with a printed version of the customer's own calculations, customized with the customer's name to take with them and review." Adding the business card of the bank's salesperson's is another nice, personal touch.

Each banking product is really a show unto itself. The bank can be viewed as a network of products, a cavalcade of shows. Each product should have its own identity or "character," just as each CSR and customer have unique characteristics. Here again, desktop presentations and "what-if" financial counseling can assist the platform staff in differentiating the bank's many products and services.

PLATFORM DILEMMAS

One of the best ways to review your own platform show is to take the perspective of a new customer. Shop your own bank. How do you feel walking through the door of one of your branches for the first time? Does the ensemble cast seem to be performing, selling, and servicing at their best? Does the platform system enhance or intrude upon the interaction between CSR and customer? Sometimes a little fine-tuning or system upgrading is all that is needed.

Ask your platform staff about their jobs and how they are doing. As far as technology is concerned, do your CSRs have (and feel comfortable with) the tools they need to excel? And, more importantly, have they been trained to use these tools to their own and the bank's best advantage? Are the benefits of bank products clearly defined for customers? Are the products backed up with professional platform-based presentations that are effective and easy to use? Does the system require heavy programmer or MIS involvement? And what is the cost of owning and operating a new system?

At Valley Bancorporation, bankers can tailor Vboss for particular applications without programmer intervention. Screen presentations can be customized to highlight the features and benefits of new products, or all products.

Rhonda S. Ellis, assistant vice president of Vboss operations, coordinates training and system utilization at 16 Valley branches. An enthusiastic evangelist, Ellis exclaimed, "Our salespeople are terrific, but there is no way they can know everything about the bank's 200 products, their rates, benefits, charges, and fees."

Valley bankers who built Vboss believe sellers of bank products and services need to demonstrate product knowledge, confidence, and credibility in face-to-face customer encounters.

Valley National Bank of Des Moines, Iowa is not affiliated with Valley Bancorporation. Mark Hodson, vice president of information technology at Valley National said, "Vboss enables CSRs to be more active—showing new product presentations, doing financial calculations, and automating document preparation." In a nutshell, the banker attributes the improvement of the quality of service as well as the delivery of information about new products to the Vboss system. "The same new product information is available to all tellers and CSRs instantly," stated Hodson.

Vboss clinics, workshops, and frequent meetings keep CSRs informed and solve problems both minor and major. Part of Ellis' job is to channel user feedback. It sure seems as if the platform staff is treated with respect, and this translates into higher product sales, satisfied customers, and better productivity—three essentials in making new products as successful as they can be, and improving the bank's bottom-line performance.

If CSRs are juggling too many responsibilities, they will drop a ball, especially at those times when the bank is busy. According to a

Puget Sound National spokesperson, "the bank is continually wrestling with the dilemma of service and sales and striking the proper balance between the two." When in doubt, the bank and its CSRs put quality service ahead of everything else.

One response to the variety and number of products, as well as the complexity of tasks and responsibilities is specialization at banks. The new platform cast includes personal banking representatives who dispense financial advice and handle the bulk of the sales activities, while the traditional CSR takes care of service and transaction duties.

The Latest in Platform Sales Tools

The platform terminal is the pivot in the person-to-person cross-sell process. As the customer service representative (CSR) views a platform terminal screen, he or she can scan the customer's entire relationship with the bank and identify services that should be brought to the customer's attention. New features and functions of branch automation systems are designed to improve the quality and efficiency of the cross-selling process, enhance personal service, and reduce the guesswork on the part of the CSR.

BRINGING IT ALL TOGETHER

The Tortoise and the Hare

There are so many different ways of implementing branch automation; a scheme and a system can work for one bank while failing to meet the needs of another institution. At Providence, Rhode Island-based Fleet/Norstar, the problems were complex to say the least. After successfully merging eight data centers in 1989, Fleet/Norstar decided to tackle the front office a year later. Of the eight separate banks, two had platform automation and six did not; only three of the eight banks had automated teller functions.

According to Dave Sheppard, executive vice president at Fleet/ Norstar Services Company, the $20 million project involved bringing 8 to 16 branches online each week. The bank selected a PC-based local area network (LAN) system from NCR Corp., after evaluating four other systems. "We liked the cost-benefit structure and wanted an off-the-shelf system that we could modify and expand to suit our anticipated needs," states Sheppard. Some would say that

Fleet/Norstar's 18-month implementation schedule for the bank's 570 branches was far from "fleet," but Sheppard defended the strategy. "We aimed to dramatically improve customer service and emphasize cross-selling tools at the platform." And the bank wanted to move at a pace that it could control.

Boston-based Shawmut National Corp. took a novel step, which appeared to be a step backward in automation. As with its superregional peer, Fleet/Norstar, Shawmut places multibank consolidation as a driving force in the plan. However, Shawmut decided to place dumb terminals instead of "intelligent" PCs on platform desktops in its 480 branches. Is there a method to this madness? Shawmut bankers believed they could achieve their goals—"a single set of systems and products"—with technology that was less complex and easier to manage.

Contrary to manufacturers' claims, there is no such thing as an "intelligent" workstation. One of the greatest marketing ploys of the modern banking era is the replacement of "dumb terminals" with "smart personal computers." Every banker simply has to have one. Trade in and trade up. However, powerful hardware has no "transforming" powers. Many banks who outfitted CSRs with 386 PCs with hard disks, color monitors, and "productivity software tools" have yet to realize the slightest strategic benefit. An executive at Bank of America, which installed 18,000 PCs throughout its statewide network, admitted, "There is nothing that we are doing right now on PCs that cannot be done using a dumb terminal."

Faced with plummeting earnings, not to mention shareholder stock shock as the market continued its downward spiral in the waning days of the 1990 calendar year, Shawmut made some other hard decisions. A bank executive stated that Shawmut will change procedures to conform to a "single off-the-shelf branch automation system." In other words, no customization needed here. Economies of scope and the low-cost road to product and system standardization may not lead to success, but at Shawmut and at many other institutions, survival is the goal.

Merger-Minded Mellon Bank

Mergers prodded Pittsburgh-based, seven-multibank **Mellon Bank** to become consolidation-minded. Merging back rooms and front-office branch delivery systems occupied Mellon managers for more than four years. In its deliberate style, Mellon brought all branches, spread across three states, into the common fold.

Dick Gallerno, vice president of retail project development at Mellon started conducting the symphonizing of the branch automation in 1986. "Mellon was a leader in automating teller tasks dating back to the late 1960s," explains Gallerno. "[The bank] also constructed and consolidated its CIFs in the early 1970s." Bankers embarking on branch automation project quickly learn the value of a consolidated CIF. One bank executive dubbed the lack of CIF integration "the black hole of branch automation."

Contrary to published reports in the banking press, Mellon was not really pursuing a McDonald's approach to retail banking. And, while quick, accurate service is desirable, frenetic, "fast food" financial decisions can be unhealthy. Mellon's strategy remains an evolutionary one, building upon and extending the existing technology base in increments to achieve retail banking and productivity goals.

Standardization of retail products was one such goal. Mellon wanted to speak in the same voice to all its customers, but the voice tells a slightly different story because product rates do vary according to market competitive conditions. Gallerno cites specific gains from the ongoing effort: "We reduced the time to open a new account by 50 percent; automated documentation enables a CSR to print as many as five separate forms from a single screen; and with editing and tutorials, CIF errors have been cut by more than 65 percent."

California Dreamin'

Bringing new automation to 16 branches a week is a bear of a task, but Bank of America pulled it off in a technological blitz that cost the bank more than $100 million.

The project involved installation of 10,000 teller workstations and 8,000 platform systems in the bank's 870 branches. BofA skillfully planned the massive project right down to the microdetails. Precise planning and synchronized coordination enabled the bank to bring all its branches online in about 18 months. Normally a branch automation project of this scope takes a minimum of three to four years to complete.

Access to customer information was vastly improved. And delivery of information and applications was tailored to the tasks at hand, according to Richard J. Clausen, vice president of retail automation. Instead of making CSRs search for a needle in a haystack when a customer asks for information about a particular product or account, the system "pricks" the CSR with the answer.

"Why PCs for all, you may ask?" pondered Clausen. "Controller-based technology works fine, but it is a 1970 technology with very obvious limitations. We chose PCs (actually IBM PS/2s) because we wanted to control the cost of future changes." Other benefits of the PC-based, LAN system included faster product implementation, longer life cycles of the equipment, a wider range of software, and easier system customization, and "application version control, so everyone is using the same software," said Clausen.

Who Goes There?

Clausen maintained that, although the branch automation system packs a lot of technology, from magnetic stripe readers to customer pin selection terminals for immediate on-site debit card enrollment, it is not "technology-driven." "The real purpose was to give tellers and CSRs the *information* to serve and sell better," explained Clausen. "You can't leave the teller out of the equation." With a swift swipe through mag stripe reader, a teller can see a complete relationship overview on the screen for the customer at the window.

Michael Bal, an executive at PNC's Provident National Bank, echoed Clausen's sentiments: "More than 90 percent of retail customers only interact with tellers." Very few banks encourage tellers to recognize or take advantage of opportunities to refer customers to a CSR for CDs or other products. "A one percent success rate in teller referrals could boost new account sales to existing customers by 15 percent," claims Bal.

If the dream is customer satisfaction and protection and growth of retail banking market share, then better customer relations and quality service must be priorities for any branch automation project. To a great extent, the system is a detail. It is the people—the customer and the bank staff—who really matter, and the process of training, retraining, and fine-tuning that make the difference after all the machines are in place and the last cable has been connected.

A Swift Operation of Epic Proportions

In branch automation, bankers tend to focus on the applications, the hardware components, which they consider to be " the brains of the system." However, the delivery of the information and applications, particularly the telecommunications aspects, are the most costly and mission-critical, particularly in large-scale projects such as **Bank of America.**

Integrating BofA's sprawling, electronic vascular branch automation network for the state of California was like installing a new nervous system in a patient the size of Gulliver. The system was actually comprised of 875 LANs that could be considered separate data centers in every lilliputian branch. Comparable projects handled in a more traditional manner would take years, but BofA set a goal of bringing the project to completion in 18 months.

"You want numbers, we got numbers," says Clausen. "We got 875 branches, a total of 1,300 locations, 7.2 million accounts with 150,000 new accounts opened monthly. We mail 6.7 million customer statements monthly and answer 1.5 million customer service calls monthly."

The operation was managed by a team of the bank's corporate real estate staff and the telecommunications services division of Flour Daniel, which provided project management, production design and engineering, and construction management services. Since the design and construction of 250 branch sites were in process at any one time, coordination and communication of activities were critical. The success of the project rested on the ability to establish an integrated statewide telecommunications backbone linking each branch LAN into the bank's three data centers. The single network consolidates 66 discrete networks installed over the last generation.

The design and construction process took an average of 16 weeks for each branch; at any one time, 14 design teams and eight test teams were busily working at branches, in addition to 100 engineers. Each week, 25 copies of construction plans for each of the 16 sites were produced and express-mailed to contractors, subcontractors, BofA managers, and government agencies; more than 130,000 drawings and 105,000 pages of documentation were produced.

The end result: a remarkably high-level of standard design and consistency among bank branches, economies from the specialization of labor, and steady production rates resulting from execution of the effort in a sequentially planned and controlled manner. The degree of detail—down to the wall plug level—which was incorporated into the planning and design phases, caused fewer on-site modifications, fewer deviations in construction, and significantly lower unit costs.

When You Wish upon a CSR

Consolidation of multibank systems is only the beginning, albeit a new beginning for many institutions. The bankers interviewed have all chosen a similar tactic to make cross-selling easier for the CSR.

So maybe one simple answer to the complexities of retail banking in the 1990s lies in "bringing everything together." It means consolidating operations, standardizing products and systems, "speaking in one voice," and delivering a relationship view of each individual customer for tellers and CSRs to see. It is a mission that is much easier to describe than achieve. For some bankers it has been a lifelong mission.

The advantages of any branch automation technology are fleeting. "You are either trying to stay ahead or catch up at any given moment," says BofA's Clausen. State-of-the-art systems that are here today must be replaced or upgraded tomorrow. The only constant is change. Some bankers see change as a form of tragedy, others call it "the challenge."

5

Electronic Banking

From automated teller machines (ATMs) and in-branch self-service strategies to interactive voice response to direct debit point-of-sale (POS), new-age electronic banking beckons every retail banker. But is technology a siren calling bankers to crash their ships against the rocks, or an automated savior that can satisfy customers and generate real revenue growth?

New-age branch banking forges electronic links between the bank and customers for anyday, anytime, anywhere service.

THE REBIRTH OF THE ATM

Let's begin with a capsule history and some current events in the deployment and usage of ATMs.

Many retail banks are entering the fourth phase of the ATM era; the evolutionary stages of ATMs can be charted according to the following developmental course:

- The **Birthing Phase** (circa 1970–1976) marked the pioneering use of ATMs by the early-adopting banks. Rapid sales to big banks created a short-lived competitive advantage. There was scant understanding of customer needs or expectations and only vague strategizing as to the role of ATMs in banks' overall retail delivery systems.

- In the **Acceptance Phase** (1977–1984) nearly every bank had to have some (ATMs) to keep up with the bank down the street. During this era, the regional switching networks also pulled bankers into participation and ATM investment. Bankers expected customers to expect the convenience of anytime and anyplace account access. However, bankers started to notice that ATMs were a drag on profits and only a third of all customers actually used the machines. New machine sales peaked in 1983, when 40,000 machines were in operation.

- During the **Maturity (and Decline?) Phase** (1984–the early 1990s) most bankers (grudgingly) accepted ATMs as a necessary cost of being in the retail banking business. The mid-1980s marked the the advent of national networks—Cirrus and Plus—placing pressures on the smaller regional alliances. Customers expected constant availability; bankers seemed satisfied with 97 percent uptime. Due to widespread market placements (machine population is forecast to hit the 100,000 mark in 1992), ATMs are generally viewed as a generic service, a commodity with no competitive advantage. ATM manufacturers begin development of next generation technologies.

Table 5–1.   ATM Usage Trends

Transaction	Volume	Trends
Banks that own or operate ATMs	83.0%	↔
Average monthly transaction volume	5,354	↓
Average withdrawal	$62.00	↔
Average deposit	$460.00	↑
Banks charging proprietary ATM fees	15.3%	↑
Banks charging interchange ATM fees	77.0%	↑
Average interchange transaction fee	$0.85	↑
Bank participation in networks	73.0%	↑
Card issuance at account opening	19.0%	↑
Households using ATM cards	51.0%	↔
Monthly use of ATMs by active users	3.1	↑

Sources: BAI ATM Usage Study 1990; Frost & Sullivan; Industry Analysts.

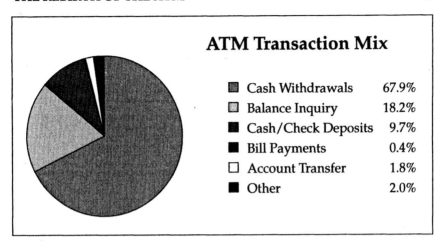

ATM Transaction Mix

▨	Cash Withdrawals	67.9%
▨	Balance Inquiry	18.2%
■	Cash/Check Deposits	9.7%
■	Bill Payments	0.4%
☐	Account Transfer	1.8%
■	Other	2.0%

Figure 5–1. ATM transaction mix. *Source:* BAI ATM Usage Study, 1990.

Bankers bemoan the low transaction volumes per machine and the fact that half of American households have never used an ATM (see Table 5–1). To most of the other half of America, ATMs are nothing more than cash-vending machines. Other trends indicate that more banks are instituting fees, partly intended to cover the ongoing machine overhead in addition to transaction interchange costs. For example, Valley Bank of Nevada charges noncustomers an electronic silver dollar for using any of the bank's more than 100 ATMs in Las Vegas casinos. But Valley will not charge its own customers for ATM use. However, analysts predict a gradual rise in the number of banks that will charge for proprietary machine use; nearly four in five banks already charge fees for network interchange transactions.

Industrywide, the share of check or cash deposits at ATMs as a part of the overall transaction mix is declining (see Figure 5–1); and only 4 of every 1,000 ATM transactions are bill payments. Many bankers (and even some of the ATM suppliers) assert that ATMs must be easier to use before customers take that leap of faith and start depositing checks and cash. To change the transaction mix and attract more ATM users requires a strategy and the automated means to make it happen.

The Fourth Dimension

The new era of the ATM will either be the *Replacement* or *Rebirth Phase*. It is starting now. The fork in the road will differentiate the ATM strategy of banks more than ever before. There are both technological and "behavioral" aspects to this turning point in automated self-services delivered via multifeatured, user-friendly ATMs.

Smart Marketing of ATMs

At CoreStates Financial Corp. and Fleet/Norstar Rhode Island, the ATM aims and activities are similar: wean customers away from tellers; reduce staff; provide superior customer self-service conveniences; and market, market, market.

CoreStates owns and operates the Money Access System (MAC) network, the industry interchange leader at 17 million plus transactions per month, far more than the national networks—MasterCard-owned *Cirrus* and Visa partially owned *Plus*—combined. MAC is the primary reason for CoreStates impressive noninterest income growth—up more than 16 percent in 1989.

Customers of the Newtown, Pennsylvania CoreStates' branch are participating in a new-age self-service retail banking experiment. The first thing you notice upon approaching the bank is a pair of drive-up ATMs; inside the branch are cash-only ATMs and an NCR Exact Cash ATM that can cash checks to the penny. The Exact Cash machine also provides proof to the customer that the check has been deposited. A receipt contains a record of the bank on which the check was drawn, the account number, sequence number of the check, and the dollar amount.

Fleet/Norstar is leveraging a superlative accomplishment of one of its member banks. The ATM program of Fleet/Norstar in Rhode Island is being dealt out to other regions. During the 1980s, Fleet/Norstar installed about 60 ATMs in Rhode Island and reduced its full-time teller staff by 70. "One-third of all customer transactions are processed by an ATM," according to A. Christian Fredrick Jr., senior vice president of products and services. ATMs in supermarkets, airports, and train stations, and on college campuses also record a high degree of noncustomer use. Bankwide, 300 ATMs log about 2 million transactions per month.

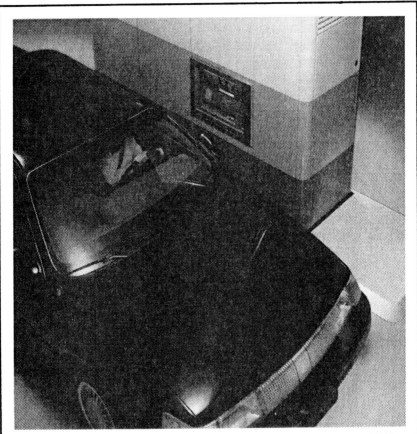

Although a new Fleet/Norstar customer receives his or her PIN by mail, the ATM card goes to the local bank branch. When the customer picks up the card, a Fleet customer representative demonstrates all its uses (withdrawals, deposits, account transfer, and bill payment) and ensures a successful initial "man-machine interface." Not surprisingly, deposits account for more than 20 percent of ATM use at Fleet/Norstar's Rhode Island branches—more than double the industry average.

Card Dealing

The secret to more effective ATM usage is changing or modifying consumer behaviors. The best time to start the change process is at the new-account opening. Most banks send an ATM card and machine-selected PIN to a new customer weeks after he or she opens an account. As of 1990, only one in five retail banks issued ATM cards on the spot at the time of the new-account opening. About one in ten banks demonstrate the use of ATMs to new customers.

Richard Wilhide, vice president of retail delivery systems at Delaware-based Wilmington Trust Company reports that the bank has issued ATM cards and PINs to new customers on the spot since 1984. CSRs demonstrate the types of transactions to ensure the first success. As a result, states Wilhide, "85 percent of our customers have ATM cards and 45 percent are active in any given month."

Bankers-in-the-know have learned that customer-selected PINs are easier to remember and as a result the ATM card is used more often. Atalla Corporation, a market leader in ATM and POS security automation, is one provider of confidential, self-selected PIN systems.

ATM Lotto

Another successful technique to modify customer behavior is sweepstakes and "pavlovian" promotions. Fleet/Norstar uses local newspaper advertising, narrow-cast radio ads, and point-of-sale promotions to attract both customers and noncustomers. In 1989, Fleet conducted a "Beat the Bank" sweepstakes; the grand-prize winner walked off with $2,600 in ATM-dispensed cash. Another Fleet/Norstar promotion involved ATMs located at Stop & Shop convenience stores. In each instance, ATM usage dropped off after the contest ended; however, *sustained* ATM usage gains still registered a healthy 8 to 9 percent.

The Hole-in-the-Wall Gang

Who are the industry leaders in ATM usage and machine deployment? Citibank makes the list; and the west coast is well-represented. Illinois-based Network EFT is not a bank but owns and operates ATMs located in Chicago food stores. In 1990, two other nonbank ATM leaders also concentrate on the supermarket arena: Publix Super Markets of Lakeland, Florida holds the number 15 spot with 475 ATMs in operation, and GTE EFT Services of Long Beach, California, ranked 17th with 470 machines in Safeway, Winn Dixie, Vons, A&P, and Hughes stores. In surveying the top 10 ATM Leaders, one bank is a surprising standout (see Table 5–2).

Table 5–2. ATM Leaders—The Top 10

Rank and Bank	ATM Supplier(s)	Total ATMs	Trans-actions Monthly (MM)	ATM Card-holders (MM)
1. BankAmerica	Diebold	1,822	17	4.0
2. First Interstate	IBM, Diebold, NCR, Docutel	1,400	11	5.5
3. Citibank	Proprietary	1,300*	9	1.5
4. Wells Fargo	IBM	1,250	10.5	2.3
4. (tie) BayBanks	Diebold, Fujitsu	1,250	11.3	.95
6. Security Pacific	IBM, Diebold, NCR	1,229	9	2.4
7. Network EFT†	Concord	1,055	.89	N/A
8. Rocky Mountain Bankcard System	IBM, Diebold, NCR	840	2.8	1.2
9. Citizens & Southern and Sovran	IBM, Diebold, Docutel, NCR	820‡	1.7‡	5.5
10. First Union and Florida National	Diebold, IBM, NCR	777‡	5.5‡	1.3

Sources: Faulkner & Gray *1990 Card Industry Directory, American Banker,* Bank 1989 Annual Reports.

N/A: Figures not available.

* Citibank also operates another 400 ATMs outside the United States.

† Owns and operates a network of cash and scrip dispensers located in Chicago food stores.

‡ Estimates based on preliminary merger information.

With $10 billion assets, BayBanks is the fourth largest bank in the northeast, yet it has more ATMs (1,250) than Fleet/Norstar, Bank of Boston, and Shawmut *combined.* Roughly one out of every two ATMs in Massachusetts belongs to Boston-based BayBanks. As the 1990s began, BayBanks was processing more monthly ATM transactions than Citibank.

According to a BayBanks spokesperson, "about 70 percent of the bank's customers use an ATM in any given month; 94 percent of all account holders have cards." In addition, BayBanks owns and operates the XPress 24 network, which has a membership of more than 100 financial institutions, including 15 credit unions. In terms of regional switch volume, at 11 million transactions a month XPress ranks second only to CoreStates' MAC.

BayBanks is not an overnight success story; a clear vision for ATMs was sketched back in 1977—a strategy that is still evolving. A spokesperson at BayBanks Inc., the bank's ATM and automation arm, believes, "we have increased retail market share by one percent annually because of our ATMs." This percentage converts to 125,000 households attracted by the convenience and services afforded by BayBanks ATMs. Not content to rest on its record, Baybanks continues to incorporate new customer services and enhancements. Recently, the bank added printed ministatements or summaries of account activity and a feature that enables customers to "preset" their usual cash withdrawal amount.

Emperor of the Hill

The world leader in ATMs is the Japanese Post Office Savings System with 6,000 ATMs and more than 10 million cardholders. Five other Japanese financial institutions rank in the top 10 in global ATM billboard. In fact, there are more ATM cards in Japan than there are Japanese.

A few other cultural differences stand out compared to ATM practices in the United States. In Japan 75 percent of all deposits are made through ATMs. An industry analyst projects that the machines have enabled banks and other financial institutions to displace or reallocate about 30 percent of the staff. And while Americans are limited to between $200 and $400 in daily cash withdrawals, the Japanese limit is about a million yen (roughly $8,000).

The other amazing phenomenon in the land of the rising sun is that all the machines close down at sunset, actually at 7 P.M., daily. Customers cannot use ATMs on Sundays or after 2 P.M. on Saturdays.

Combating ATM Fatigue

The root cause of ATM malaise in retail banking is that hardly anyone seems to care. In a 1990 *Bank Administration Institute* survey, only a scant seven out of every 100 retail bankers said they *plan* to market ATM services to increase or incent customer usage. Popular wisdom indicates that if seven bankers say they plan to do something, two or three will actually follow through.

At thousands of banks across the country, no one is responsible or wants to be associated with the loss-leading black boxes in the wall. Unless ATM are championed and managed and marketed, don't expect usage patterns to change. If you do nothing you have nothing to gain. CoreStates, Fleet/Norstar, Wilmington Trust, BayBanks, and others are glowing institutional exceptions to the rule.

ATM Offspring

Among the innovative new uses of these old black boxes are: distribution of unemployment benefits in the state of Washington; ski-lift tickets dispensed by state-owned and operated ATMs in New Hampshire, and even postage stamp-dispensing ATMs. Dispensers that spew forth tens and twentys can be filled with many other items, including airline tickets, movie theater admission passes, and concession stand vouchers.

Paycheck cashing machines from NCR dispense bills and coins, and the new breed of Interactive Platform Machines, or the "CSR in a Box," can be installed in a bank lobby kiosk. The self-service system captures prospect data allowing the bank to follow up leads with cross-selling.

Upon closer examination, it would seem as if bankers have barely scratched the surface in ATM possibilities. In September 1990, Security Pacific Bank of Washington became the first to install ATMs that "communicate" in seven languages on the screen. At Seattle International Airport, travelers can transact in Chinese, Japanese, Korean, Russian, German, Spanish, and hometown English. A new NCR ATM, currently in testing, actually talks, guiding the user with prerecorded instructions. In a 1990 speech before the Consumer Banking Association, BankAmerica chairman and CEO Richard M. Rosenberg observed, "Branch banking is changing. The cornerstone of the bank branch will be the staid, old, tried-and-true, boring ATM." Rosenberg also envisions "smaller, stripped-down, low-cost (branch) facilities that use technology to provide the high level of service that customers demand." Alongside the boring ATM, the next technology for bankers to exploit for retail banking is the ubiquitous telephone.

AUTOMATED VOICE RESPONSE

"Press 1" for Customer Caller Profiles

At many financial institutions, the responsibility for automated or interactive voice response (IVR) systems falls under the same executive(s) charged with ATM operations. On the surface, there are many similarities between the two technologies. Both involve automation, enable customers to serve themselves, and perform many of the same account functions. IVR and ATM user profiles are nearly identical: young, affluent, and urban.

In May 1990, the ICR Survey Research Group performed a study polling both customers and bankers. Among the findings: 81 percent of those under 35 believed that banking by phone would be more convenient; 76 percent with incomes of $50,000 and up; and 72 percent of women were interested in telebanking. Urban dwellers were more interested than their country cousins; a fact confirmed by another 1990 survey, the Unidex Report. Regionally speaking, Midwesterners find telebanking most appealing while Northeasterners rate it least appealing, according to Unidex.

Telebanking callers are like ATM users in other ways. For 20 years bankers have been stymied by low customer usage of ATMs, and the same grumbling is now heard about IVR users. On average, about 13 percent of a bank's retail customers use telebanking where it is offered. However, these users appear to be frequent callers similar to the active ATM-using crowd. Some bankers who have installed IVR systems shrug their shoulders about the statistics. They are satisfied with the substantial cost savings and the ability to free employees from the drudgery of dispensing routine account answers.

At America First Credit Union in Ogden, Utah, a voice response system handles 300,000 member calls a month. "AccessLine provides deposit and savings account balances, checks recently cleared, credit card information, and funds transfer functions, on demand 24 hours a day, seven days a week," says Glenda Burnside, manager of ATM services with responsibility for the Accessline program. Burnside estimates that about 25 percent of the CU's 152,000 members make active use of the service. She also reports "savings of $240,000 since the system was first installed in 1987."

The 500-Line Gorilla

Fidelity Investments, the largest mutual funds company in America, has fused computers and communications to best serve six million customers and their information needs. Named by *Fortune* and other publications as a premier customer service organization, Fidelity fields nearly 50,000 customer calls daily, and has invested millions of dollars in a 500-line, mainframe-based IVR system since it launched the Fidelity Automated Service Telephone (FAST) in 1983. Although the system receives a million calls a month, "only 10 percent of Fidelity's customers have used FAST," reported Stuart Greenburg, vice president of strategic business systems for Fidelity Investments. Fidelity's human telephone representatives—some 1,000 around the country—work around the clock.

Customers can perform any of 120 fund-filled functions using FAST, including hourly fund pricing, account balances, interfund exchanges, redemptions, and other investment transactions. Greenburg identifies "improved speech quality, 'user-friendly' enhancements, and additional information services" as key requirements to expand customer usage in the 1990s.

The booming market for voice processing systems and services topped one billion dollars in 1990, with banking and the financial services industries accounting for the lion's share of new system installations. In 1987, voice response systems were installed in a mere 3 percent of financial institutions; by 1990, 47 percent of all banks had embraced the technology.

Voice Technology Comes of Age

The personal computer has actually been the impetus behind burgeoning telebanking. Automated voice response systems have been on the scene for nearly 20 years, but only as big computer, high-ticket luxury items suitable for only the largest banks. The advent of PC-based systems have put the technology well within the reach of the common bank.

George Mattingly, a director at First Union Bank has been involved with voice technology since its infancy in the 1960s. He recalls when "tellers were the only users of voice response. They could get to the customer account file on the host computer and perform a variety of inquiry and transaction functions." Tellers at about half of First Union's branches still utilize telephone-based connection to the bank's mainframe.

An executive vice president of Syntellect, Inc., a supplier of PC-based voice response systems, points out that IVR systems "have probably replaced 250,000 operators who used to sit in front of terminals or computer screens and read data to customers on the phone, and created jobs for another 500,000 automated operators." However, IVR and other voice-based technologies go far beyond simple automation to "informate" communications and interactions between the bank and its retail customers, among the bank's co-workers, and even among the bank's diverse information systems.

Voice systems appear in many guises. Although IVR is the most widely embraced system for customer teleservicing, other offspring of the blissful union between telecommunications and computers include predictive dialers for automated, outbound calling functions for credit collections and telemarketing, voice mail and messaging, and audiotext or announcement services to provide loan and CD rate quotes.

Other reasons spurring adoption of IVR are the deregulation of the telephone industry and the universal availability of Touch-Tone phones. The beeps and boops of the Touch-Tone phone are music to the ears of a computer—a digital language for data exchange. The phone becomes, in effect, a computer terminal in the hands of customers.

Advances in speech synthesis have also contributed to the rapid rise of IVR. In days of yore these systems spoke in alien machine-like voices. Today, the bank can record and store a real human voice that greets callers in easy-to-understand speech, and converses with customers in a natural, hometown dialect from the "yawls" of Southern Belle Bank, to the haard "a's" of First Beantown S&L. One of the first multilingual voice response systems, installed at the Air Defense Center Federal Credit Union in Fort Bliss, Texas, serves 92,000 members, including service personnel around the world. The system provides account information in the caller's choice of English, Spanish, and German.

The Resurrection of Home Banking

Remember home banking? Retail bankers who tried to link customers' personal computers to the bank's mainframe probably wish they didn't.

PC-based home banking was a whirlpool fiasco for the pioneers who tested the waters in the mid-1980s. In fact, Banc One tried and failed twice, but is about to attempt a third PC-based home banking system. In late 1990, after years of sluggish use, Chase Manhattan's home banking program was about to be evicted from the the bank's roster of customer services.

IVR systems spearhead the new home banking movement. The telephone keypad has replaced the PC keyboard. Aside from the anytime, anywhere convenience of telebanking, there is no need to provide any special software for the customer. Everyone has the hardware. A user only needs to lift the telephone handset and push the buttons. How much easier can it get?

Another clear benefit for the bank is the payback. IVR systems pay for themselves in as little as four months time. Compare that to ATMs. And with voice response systems there are no "unsightly holes in the wall."

Is there a downside risk to this new high-tech, tele-thing? Not according to the bankers, who are nearly unanimous in their praise of voice response systems. Many banks are extending their IVR systems by adding new applications and account information due to the overwhelmingly positive reception by customers.

Advantages

Of the many advantages of IVR, the best news is that it gives bankers the ability to control and manage incoming customer telephone traffic. It virtually eliminates those constant interruptions that bring staff productivity to a grinding halt in response to callers' routine inquiries. An IVR system controls this labor-intensive process. According to bankers, the typical telephone inquiry requires about 10–15 minutes to answer by an operator, some customer calls run as long as 30 minutes even though little information is being provided. It is mostly friendly conversation. Voice response eliminates chitchat and efficiently gets the job done. And while the typical cost of a telephone inquiry handled by an operator is $1.50 or more, that answered by a voice response system is a quarter or less.

A voice response system emulates an operator or CSR who answers customer calls, manually keystrokes inquiries into the host computer terminal, and reads the answers from a CRT screen. On the other end of the telephone line, customers hear a friendly, human voice that greets the caller, guides him or her through every step of the process, servicing their needs swiftly and accurately. This automated operator never calls in sick or takes vacations. It is "on call" 24 hours a day, seven days a week if you desire. Customers who are shy about asking for their account balance from a bank employee also appreciate the privacy of a voice response system. These systems also provide the option to transfer calls requiring assistance to a live operator during business hours. The bank can structure and tailor the system to meet particular requirements and servicing needs.

At Union Bank in Newport Beach, California, an IVR system aids in handling customers' calls. "Before the system was installed, the bank needed 13 operators to handle 400 daily calls," according to a Union Bank senior VP. After the system was installed, the bank retained two part-time phone people to provide special customer assistance. The system paid for itself in nine months. A measure of the system's popularity is that, while 25 percent of the bank's customers use ATMs, nearly 75 percent have used voice response to perform their banking chores.

Another innovative application is the use of a voice response as a backup to ATM service. A few banks have linked phones in ATM locations to their voice response system so customers can still get answers to their account questions and perform funds transfers if the ATM is temporarily out of service.

More Than an Automated TellerPhone Machine

At Hollywood Federal, a $1.3 billion savings and loan in Hollywood, Florida, Touch-Tone bill payment originated at the bank in 1978 with an audio response unit from IBM. Customer acceptance soon strained the limits of the system and Hollywood Federal switched to a minicomputer system. The bank's vice president of payment systems cites an average of $50K a month in profit from the bill payment service, called "Bill-O-Matic," which serves 25,000 account holders and over 85,000 merchants nationwide. In addition to the cost savings in overhead and staffing, the bank generates fee-income by charging 15 cents per telephone transaction—which is (as of 1992) 14 cents less than paying by mail. In general, bankers are leery of telephone bill paying. Most are content to wait until voice response achieves a certain level of customer acceptance before venturing into bill payment or other fee-based services that involve heavy backroom support.

How It Happens

Let's take a look at the general operating features of these systems. They all provide easy hookup to the bank's host computer, digitized human speech, lightening-fast caller response time, access from any Touch-Tone phone, and can be expanded or networked to accommodate increased call volume. In addition, all the systems are easily trainable in speech response. You select an employee or a "professional" actor to record the spoken responses to customer callers. The recording can be done in a day; programming links to host computer databases usually require a few weeks.

For retail banking applications, you select the information, such as customers' account balances, and interest paid/earned year to date. These "DDA fields" in the core system are then tagged. When a customer calls, the system "fishes" for the online data, hooks it, and reels it in to the IVR system. It then tells the size, or amount, of the "catch" to the customer. While customers are fishing for answers, you can monitor their activity and exploit the information about system use as a strategic tool for luring customers to the bank's new products and fee-based services.

Any computer-connected IVR system can be programmed to capture valuable call data. Each and every contact can be automatically logged to determine caller characteristics and trends in customer usage. Voice response systems can inconspicuously canvass callers to solicit interest in new bank products, such as mortgage and car loans, CDs, and investment vehicles. Banks using voice response to test new products report some interesting results. When a caller to California First Bank selects "News About Services" he or she hears a brief audio commercial for the latest bank product promotion. If interested, and the call is placed during banking hours, the customer can be immediately transferred to a waiting CSR. Another feature of this interactive system is the ability to get not only loan rate information, but the monthly payments and APR information on loans just by keying in the desired amount.

Trends

Software breakthroughs, such as integrated voice-fax, matched with advances in telecommunications, voice/data workstations, and improved connectivity among diverse customer databases and computer systems, portend an enriched menu of choices for bankers to ponder, as shown in the following list.

10 Top "Chatterbox" Applications in Banking

1. Automated voice response provides checking and savings account information to call-in customers at more than 7,000 financial institutions.
2. Autodialing and predictive dialing streamlines the collections process to nab lazy and delinquent customers.
3. Voice mail and messaging systems enable employees to keep informed and eliminate telephone tag.
4. Audiotext and announcement systems broadcast ATM locations, branch hours of operation, and investment and loan rates.
5. Credit card authorizations and customer services to report lost or stolen cards at any time.
6. Cash management services by phone, such as balance reporting, informate fee-based banking services attractive to the burgeoning small-business market.
7. Automated funds transfer by phone make electronic moves between accounts as easy as can beep.
8. Inbound/outbound telemarketing systems combine teleservicing with telesales for teleconvenience and teleprofits.
9. Emerging voice/fax applications for mortgage and auto lending as well as instant delivery of bank statements.
10. Integrated voice–data–text–image or "multimedia telebanking" opens the door to a wide range of internal, networked applications and customer products and services.

There are more than 100 uses for telephonic, online banking services and products, far more than can be addressed in a few pages. Yet it is possible to define opportunities—communication channels that bring the bank to the customer—for every banker.

Big Banks' Big Plans

Wells Fargo Bank has had a change of mind with respect to telebanking. In 1987, the San Francisco bank proclaimed in newspaper advertisements that customers could call at any time and talk with the bank

"Person-to-Person." In 1990, Wells Fargo installed a small army of INFOBOTs, Syntellect's IVR device, to handle a portion of 100,000 daily customer calls. The typically tight-lipped bank would not reveal the customer usage of the automated service; and stresses that real people are still available to answer calls in addition to the computerized informants. But since Wells Fargo has 600 incoming lines for automated telebanking (and a reliable source claimed another 200 would be added by 1991), one must assume that quite a few West Coast callers prefer the Touch-Tone alternative.

Heading across country, telebanking has Touch-Toned a nerve at a number of Manhatten's money center banks. Chemical Bank, a long-time user of telebanking, started with 6,000 calls daily and now gets 40,000. Plans are afoot to answer as many as 100,000 customer calls using a 400-line system.

ET Phone Home (Banking)

Citibank intends to use its own custom-designed phone to provide standard telebanking and resuscitate automated bill payments. The device is in the testing phase with a few hundred hand-picked customers. "E.T.," for Enhanced Telephone, was developed by the bank's own Transaction Technology, Inc. division and is being manufactured to Citibank's specifications by the Dutch electronics giant Philips International.

In 1990, pilot tests with 400 hand-picked customers, funds transfers were among the most performed task. The test also uncovered consumer interest in stock and bond quotes.

E.T. looks like a typical desk phone except for a small, built-in screen display above the keypad and a hidden keyboard underneath that is used to enter the names of companies for bill payment or other textual account information. Connections for a printer and/or a fax machine are contained in the back of the device. If all goes well, the Citibank party line could grow to a million by the end of the mid-1990s.

The true measure of success of any home banking or phone banking system is not hardware or the "delivery device," rather it is the applications and functions that customers use or expect, and the benefits reaped by the bank's business units or departments. How do banks go about defining the right package of services and information to enable and encourage customers to help themselves?

Over the years Chase Manhattan Bank has installed a variety of IVR systems. By mid-1990, "the bank has voice systems from five different suppliers—from mainframe- to mini- to PC-based," reports a Chase vice president. Separate systems "informate" applications in cash management, corporate money transfer, credit card customer services, merchant authorization, and inbound collections. A brand-new replacement system is now online to bolster consumer telebanking. Chase has incorporated "Pay by Phone" bill payment into the existing roster of retail telebanking services. Data are retrieved from two different host systems—one for account information and another for bill payments. Chase began with 88 telephone lines, but the system can easily grow to 256 lines should telephone traffic warrant.

At Chase, standardization is an important issue. "There has been a proliferation of needs, applications, and systems; we don't want to assume the decision-making for the business units but we do want to provide a framework to guide selection," states a bank spokesperson.

Super Information Servers

Voice systems are evolving into "dedicated information servers" that fit into multivendor computer environments and handle multiple telebanking applications. Voice "gateways" to a range of computer-stored information, and applications offer new solutions for customer products and services and the opportunity to design and implement a coordinated, multimedia telebanking system.

In a truly interactive fashion, a customer could call the bank's IVR system, which would ask questions to prequalify the caller for a car loan. The system could then send a partially completed application via fax to the car dealer or directly to the consumer. This does more than automate the delivery of an automobile loan application, it actually expedites the lending process, improves customer service, and creates a competitive advantage for both the dealership and the lending institution. It also puts the driver behind the wheel in record time.

In another stretch of voice technology, Adaptive Information Systems (AIS) and Syntellect are jointly exploring voice and image integration. A component of the AIS system provides remote access via regular telephone lines to information and images stored on optical disk.

Document images and other information can be sent to the user's choice of fax or PC. Touch-Tone applications in development include mortgage lending and investment fund and trust management. For a mortgage loan closing, the system can gather loan payoff and tax data on demand, extract the information from multiple host computers, place the data in the proper fields on loan documents, and send the "electronic folder" to a fax machine, or to a PC with a laser printer, in an attorney's office. This reduces the process from about a week of paper shuffling and folder routing to under 10 minutes.

When autodialing is linked with an IVR system, bankers can deliver recorded reminders to customers who are as few as five days late with their credit card or installment loan payments. The entire process is completely hands- or operator-free. An IVR unit can record a customer's "spoken" promise to pay or request a payment date and amount information by Touch-Tone input. At Chase Manhattan, the collections IVR system asks the customer to provide the last payment date and check information.

When Automatic Number Identification (ANI) is linked to an inbound automatic call distributor, a delinquent customer calling the bank can be identified by his or her phone number, immediately routed to a collections agent while the system retrieves the customer's file to hit the collector's screen at the same time the call is answered. This may sound like science fiction, but such a system is being tested at more than one financial institution.

Crystal Ball Predictions

In the past, many IVR systems were proprietary. Getting systems to communicate interactively was like trying to mate a cat and a dog. New systems are more compatible, or they are single-source solutions. Integrated platform for coordinated call and voice processing incorporate IVR with voice messaging, audiotext, autoattendant, and outbound call processing. Banks can build an integrated system module by module or launch an entire package of telebanking services.

Advances in open systems architecture are also fueling integrated telebanking applications. In the not so distant future, fiber optics and broadband telecommunications will make multimedia telebanking applications practical and cost effective. Banks and their IVR suppliers will create new crossroads, new intersections of telephonic solutions. Integrated inbound/outbound telemarketing, linked with the bank's marketing customer information file system, is one area ripe for development.

While some bankers ponder the future, others are seizing the moment and installing or testing integrated, interactive telebanking. They are racing ahead to meet customers' needs and create valuable, information-rich teleproducts and teleservices.

DEBIT CARDS AND POINT-OF-SALE STRATEGIES

Direct debit point of sale (POS) payment tends to bewilder most bankers. Although debit payment processing has been practiced with limited success by some of the major players since 1987, to most bankers debit POS is a spectator sport. They are unsure of how to participate in or support multipayment options with an enhanced ATM/debit card or a double-duty debit/credit bankcard. After all, cash, checks, and credit cards seem to be excellent forms of payment, so why invest in more technology if the payoffs are not substantial, or at least assured. Retail bank executives must strategically master the economics of a direct debit POS program as well as provide the requisite marketing, operations, and merchant support.

Even pioneering bankers admit the uncertainty of the short-term benefits, although they remain hopeful about longer-term competitive advantages. According to Harrison Marks, senior project manager for POS at Wachovia Bank and Trust, "Direct debit POS is unlikely to make positive contribution to a bank's bottom line for several years. The fact that a service is technologically feasible does not make it desirable or necessary."

Tender Moments

Are POS transactions fundamentally a "merchant" service? Bankers reason that when a customer is at any point of sale, he or she is acting as a merchant's customer not as a bank customer. Direct debit is most like check guarantee and the benefits for customer and merchant alike must be positioned and promoted in the same fashion, say one faction of bankers. Others consider debit POS as a bankcard enhancement for the customer, and wish to apply the same rules for merchant processing. However, of the three parties involved in each debit transaction—the customer, bank, and merchant—each seems to think that the other two benefit the most.

On one important issue, retail bankers tend to agree. When asked about the necessary retailers to make debit POS work, bankers name supermarkets, fast food restaurants, and convenience stores, with video stores and movie theater chains also appearing on some of the bankers' merchant must-lists.

Of the $450 million in checks written at the point of sale annually, more than 43 percent are done in the checkout lanes of supermarkets. A 1990 Citicorp study calculated the average sale and times per type of transaction in the supermarket (see Table 5–3).

Table 5–3. Supermarket Timing and Tender

Average Sale	Payment Type	Transaction Time (in seconds)
$11.00	Cash	15–30
$46.00	ACH Direct Debit	20–50
$46.00	Credit Card	25–30
$26.00	Check	45–90

Transaction Data Served Deluxe

Dierbergs, a Minnesota-based supermarket chain, has 20 POS terminals in 13 stores. Dierbergs has an estimated 400,000 check cashing cards in circulation and now honors the Bankmate ATM card for grocery purchases. All card transactions are processed by Deluxe Data, which not only processes the transaction but throws in the demographics on shopper profiles to boot. The demographics—age, address, income, family size, etc.—come from check cashing card data provided by supermarket shoppers. Ninety percent of Dierbergs regular shoppers carry a card. Inactive cardholders get coupons for free food and product discounts to bring customers back to the aisles.

The only shortcoming of the Deluxe Data program is the fact that they cannot currently capture merchandise data from product UPC codes.

There is some early evidence that plastic-based POS payments are settling in at supermarkets. Ernst & Young found only 6,800 POS terminals in supermarket lanes in 1987, but the number had soared more than fourfold to 28,000 by 1990. At the same time, monthly transaction volumes grew from 2.1 million to nearly 10 million. Supermarkets account for nearly two-thirds of all debit terminals and transactions (see Table 5–4).

Table 5–4. POS Terminals and Transactions 1985–1993

Year	Debit Cards (MM)	Terminals (M)	Monthly Transactions (MM)
1985	130	6.3	N/A
1987	152	25.2	3
1989	180	45.9	9.2
1993*	212	75–90	22–37

Sources: Faulkner & Gray, *POS News,* Ernst & Young.
*1993 Average of Industry Estimates.

Debit POS is also a geographic or regional phenomena. Banks and their merchant partners on the west coast and in the southeast have been more successful or at least more adventurous that those in the northeast. A quartet of Ohio banks—Fifth Third Bank, Banc One, Central Trust and Ameritrust—are among the top ten in POS transactions (see Table 5–5). Other isolated instances of successful pilots appear periodically in the press. Bankers note: *as of late 1990 all successful pilots had a merchant champion leading the debit charge.*

A vice president for cash management services at Citibank believes debit POS should be considered as part of an *integrated payment platform* including ACH debit, online debit, check verification/authorization, credit card payment, and even electronic benefits transfer (EBT).

Enriched Transaction Data

Is there a fee-income potential in enriched POS data? Bank pioneers and POS device providers cite inventory management as well as cash management as a side-benefit of this emerging technology. Administrative functions such as time and attendance tracking, are built into some devices; and individual and store productivity can be assessed because most systems require employees to log on and off the system. Electronic mail services can also be transmitted via POS terminals. The question is will merchants pay bankers for this "optional" data or will they expect the feedback and functions to come as part of the standard debit POS package.

Table 5–5. Debit POS Leaders—The Top 10 In Transactions

Institution/Headquarters	Total POS Terminals	Monthly Transactions (000)
Wells Fargo/San Francisco, CA	4,000	3,000
Security Pacific/Los Angeles, CA	2,000	1,000
Publix Super Markets/Lakeland, FL	1,992	456
Fifth Third Bank/Cincinnati, OH	86	209
BancOne/Columbus, OH	137	110
Central Trust Co./Cincinnati, OH	600	72
Alaska USA FCU/Anchorage, AL	300	23
Davenport Bank & Trust/Davenport, IA	150	20
Bank South/Atlanta, GA	1,000	8
First Tennesee Bank/Memphis, TN	1,250	3
Ameritrust Corp./Cleveland, OH	600	1

Sources: Faulkner & Gray 1990 Card Industry Directory, Bank Annual Reports.

The pot of gold at the end of the POS rainbow seems mighty speculative. Consider the customer and merchant motivation. Is convenience a strong incentive to change buying habits? Can merchants use debit POS to foster shopper loyalty, deliver frequent shopping bonuses in the form of electronic coupons and rebates. Is debit POS an essential part of new age retailing with interactive marketing and talking electronic shelf tags? Will any of these make a difference to banker's bottom lines?

Weighing the Risks and Rewards

In order to succeed debit POS must provide answers rather than questions. Debit POS must displace a percentage of one or more of the other payment formats. It must carve into credit card use, especially for those who pay their entire balance at the end of each month. The kicker here is if the customer uses a credit card with a 25 or 28 day grace period, why should he or she pay on the spot.

Displacing checks does offer some bank advantages, but customers like the payment record that check statements provide; POS payment should appear with the same detail as ATM transactions plus the merchant listing.

To be successful, one must displace cash. Bankers must look at their communities and target customers—supermarkets, fast food, and high-volume low dollar merchants, convenience stores, theaters, video chains. The benefit the banker must sell to the merchant is that debit payers seem to spend more than cash-carrying customers.

Retail and wholesale banking executives must work together to make direct debit POS work. The merchant is an important part of the overall equation. Debit POS is actually a form of cash management services for merchants as well as a payment option for customers. For example, if the bank is shooting for a major supermarket or regional fast food restaurant chain for a corporate client, then debit POS may be an element in the overall strategy. Otherwise bankers may decide to steer clear of POS for the time being. Pioneering can be costly and frustrating.

6

Innovative Imaged Products and Services

While some bankers bemoan the failures of technology to deliver sustainable strategic advantages, others warmly embrace each new breakthrough in automation. Without question, the hottest, high-tech innovation in recent memory is image processing. Image, in various guises and systems, has been on the banking scene for years; however, it is the maturing and convergence of a number of technologies that has propelled *integrated* image processing into the spotlight.

Most industry analysts believe bankers' ardor for image is real; and numerous surveys confirm the image infatuation. For example, in a Bank Administration Institute survey of billion dollar plus asset institutions, nearly 60 percent of the respondents indicated plans to install check image processing by 1993. However, times have changed and the strains of economics have curtailed or at least rescheduled many bankers' plans.

From high-volume, high-speed check and bankcard processing to applications in consumer lending to low-speed, departmental document processing, nearly everywhere you look there is an imaging alternative. Image has rapidly evolved from stand-alone, experimental, and proprietary systems of the mid-1980s into maturing, modular applications that conform to emerging standards, run on open platforms and a variety of local area networks, and take advantage of the bank's existing investments in technology to form a more harmonious processing union.

FIRST ENCOUNTERS WITH IMAGE

Bankers' first affairs with image tended to be isolated, piecemeal encounters—lots of enthusiasm, but long-term commitment was lacking. Using scanning equipment and optical disk storage, bankers bonded with image as a paper replacement and swiftly realized cost and space savings. At large financial institutions, image-based signature verification has increased back room productivity and, in certain cases, improved front office customer service.

For bankers who believe that all image systems share the same core technologies and attributes, here is a short guide to the touch and feel of image systems:

> Be alert to *hard* versus *soft* images. Older, first-generation image systems used scanners to capture a picture of a document. Many of these systems create a hard image comparable to microfilm or a photograph. Although it may be suitable for a particular storage application, such as signature verification, it is a static image carved in silicon that cannot be modified or easily manipulated; hard images tend to have limited indexing options for subsequent retrieval.

> Soft images, on the other hand, are flexible and dynamic. They can be manipulated, electronically signed or stamped for approval, combined with text, data, or voice annotations, and modified. With system tools, soft image information can be arranged into electronic file folders and automatically indexed and cross-referenced for use in a relational database.

TAMING THE PAPER TIGER

The online data processing center of the typical bank manages about 10 percent of the bank's business information. The rest of the information is stored "offline"; five percent resides in microform (either microfilm or microfiche), 85 percent is paper.

It is no revelation that banks are burdened with mountains of reports, letters, memos, contracts, receipts, checks, disclosure agreements, computer printouts—and let's not forget those ubiquitous forms. The typical financial institution, if there is such a place, may utilize about 250 different form documents for a wide range of applications. Big retail banks are known to use more than 1,000 types of forms. Some financial forms facilitate the sale of products, others register compliance with governmental regulations, still others document transactions and customer services, and the list goes on and on.

Paper Bottlenecks and Document Shuffling

Every week, everyone embarks on a paper chase to find a lost file, or is it merely a file in transit or one that is buried on someone's desk? The cost of finding routed documents is frequently estimated at $25 per search. Lost documents cost $120 or more to replicate. Executives waste two hours a week looking for a mislaid pieces of paper; executives' assistants spend five hours or more.

Paper is a space hog. And space is money. After Exchange National Bank of Chicago installed an optical disk storage system, the bank realized a net gain of nearly 1,200 square feet of office space worth $25.50 per square foot or $30,000 annually.

At most retail banks, hours are spent and misspent in document processing, data reentry, retyping to correct errors, collation, decollation, copying, routing through the interoffice mail, and faxing, filing, retrieval, and refiling. Blank forms inventory is a major job in itself. Paper wastes time, saps productivity, and is a boondoggle of the banker's daily business.

Will the WORM Eat the Fiche?

WORM (Write Once Read Many Times) optical disk storage systems are beginning to burrow into banks. They offer better and faster access to information and are especially attractive as microform alternatives for archival storage. However, they do not automate document preparation or processing. The potential of automated documents goes far beyond records management, far beyond a paper storage alternative.

Starting in the mid-1950s, around the time of the hoola hoop and Sputnik, technology started to impact everyday work at retail banks. Time-consuming, repetitive data-processing tasks, such as payroll and accounting, reaped bountiful benefits from computerization of data and text. With each new development and enhancement, banks (theoretically) could realize greater gains in white-collar worker productivity, improve service, and reduce the "skill sets" required of bank staff. Wang Laboratories calls this era, roughly from 1955 to 1985, the first era of *Knowledge Work Automation*.

Wang identifies integrated image processing as the linchpin of the second era of Knowledge Work Automation. Knowledge work falls into two main components: "getting ready," and "main work." Main work revolves around evaluating, analyzing, and making decisions on information that has been structured or prepared for review. In contrast, getting ready is the collecting and structuring of information in order to do main work. This interactive preparation phase involves processing paper documents and voice communications initiated by an event. Getting ready work is highly interactive and process-oriented.

The convergence of separate technologies—personal computers, imaging, forms software, relational databases, high-speed laser printers, and local area networking—offer a path to a total solution, a master plan to venture boldly into integrated document applications. A bevy of bankers believe document automation is *transforming* entire processes and policies and operations. What are the bottom line competitive advantages? What are some of the success stories? Let's look at some specific examples on a department by department basis.

Departmental Documents

Automated documents clearly benefit departmental applications where "workgroup solutions" are required. Not only does the group work more productively, but staff can share or recall customer information to expedite any task. One opportunity for time and labor savings is the sale or cross-sell of a new product to an existing customer. Every new product sale requires document preparation to some extent.

At Valley Banks (in Wisconsin), integrated document preparation enables the staff to quickly service the customer after a new product— be it a consumer loan, IRA, mortgage, or whatever—is sold. Paperwork for a consumer loan typically takes about 20 minutes to prepare; Vboss helps Valley Bank CSRs to get it done in two and a half minutes. Automated mortgage systems can eat up three hours in printing all the requisite forms. Valley Bank mortgage officers have all the forms ready for the customer in less than a half-hour, using the branch automation system.

Small size does not preclude smart banking, nor does size prohibit adoption of advanced technologies. With $240 million in assets, Eastern Heights State Bank, a St. Paul, Minnesota institution owned by the 3M Corporation, operates only two branches. Eastern Heights automated platform operations in 1986. Jenine Nordquist, assistant vice president of operations recalled, "Within a week of system installation, CSRs were asking to get rid of their typewriters. They didn't need them anymore."

It took about a month to design and develop the documents needed for checking and savings accounts, IRAs, and CDs. For consumer and mortgage loan products, about 80 percent of the documentation is automated. "We must still prepare some of the state and local documents because of the particular format or sequence of financial calculations that tend to vary state by state," explained Nordquist.

"Most forms companies haven't caught up in certain areas, like home equity lines of credit. We can and do design new documents in an hour," stated Nordquist. New documents can be created and existing forms can be revised quickly without programming involvement.

Eastern Heights' platform automation system automatically identifies all the documents that must be prepared to complete a transaction. Blank documents are inserted into a desktop laser printer. After the documents are presented to the customer for signature, new-account information is automatically transmitted to the host computer files. The time to prepare and process paperwork for a consumer loan can be cut from about 20 minutes to four minutes. In addition to customary forms, cashier's checks, money orders, savings bonds, follow-up letters, and many other items not typically thought of as documentation can be produced and printed through the system.

Mortgage Lending POS Abilities

According to the Mortgage Bankers Association, the average bank needs nearly 45 days to approve a mortgage application. However, instead of a month and a half, some banks can do it in a week and a half without sacrificing information or sound decision-making. They get off to a flying start with integrated document automation at the point of sale.

Loan officers using a laptop PC equipped with a modem can call for an instant credit report and receive all relevant data within a mere

40 seconds. Captured information is automatically entered on software-based forms that are programmed to perform the required calculations. The process of prequalifying a mortgage applicant can be done, *with confidence,* within 15 minutes.

In frosty Minneapolis, Minnesota, a handful of loan officers at Marquette Bank produce between 80 and 100 new loans monthly, according to vice president and manager of residential mortgages Forrest J. Gillson. "Now our processors are processors instead of typists," stated Gillson. "It takes about 10 to 15 minutes more to take application information on a laptop, but you end up saving hours in processing. Plus, its extremely efficient, cuts down on the errors, and is much more professional." Officers fill in and print the forms—loan application, verification of employment, verification of deposit, truth in lending, and good faith estimate—on site. Doug Gallagher, creator of the system added, "Another benefit is the ability to downstream information, including loan type, term, rate, points, and lock-in term, to the secondary marketing department."

The program, from Gallagher Financial Systems, has enabled other lenders to make prodigious strides in productivity. After the first year of using the system, Pittsburgh-based FirstSouth Savings Association increased loan volume 254 percent while reducing back room processing time from nearly a month to 10 days. Commonwealth Mortgage Corporation of Massachusetts put the laptop system in the hands of 100 home loan officers.

Gillson conducted a thorough search for an automated mortgage origination system. "We looked at a lot of systems; what impressed us most was . . . it worked. It did everything. It's the way mortgage banking should be run." Marquette designed some of their own forms for the system. Added Gillson, "Gallagher always sends us software form changes and updates well in advance of new regulations."

In a way, automated documents are a technological twist on mergers and acquisitions. They illustrate the potential for the successful merger of diverse automation—imaging, forms software, relational databases, high-speed laser printers, and local and wide area networking communications. And they require due diligence and innovative acquisition of information that often resides in systems and departments dispersed throughout the bank.

Automated Documents of the Future

A network-based document processing system called Viewstar is a system built for the future. It is designed for *workflow*-intensive applications that may involve any combination of multimedia (paper, image, text, data, and voice) information. For retail banking applications, very complex workflows can be built incrementally and maintained with relative ease.

By utilizing advanced technologies, including relational database management and expert systems, Viewstar's electronic documents allow any functions that can be performed on or to a paper page, such as document markup, and online annotation and highlighting. It also supports the "intelligent document"—one that is embedded with knowledge of its ownership, interrelationships, and "rules of participation."

If integrated automated documents are being discussed at your bank you may want to mull over a few preliminaries before forging ahead. One banker advised preserving and building upon the bank's existing technology, particularly PCs and network communications. He also cautioned, "Focus on systems that can handle multipurpose information processing needs. And avoid proprietary software and hardware."

Consider starting by automating documents in a startup business unit. Bankers with a success under their belt are already moving ahead to install their second application-specific document system. Chemical Bank uses image-based document processing for credit card application processing, credit card service, and statement processing. New systems are planned for credit card collection and in the student loan area. One other suggestion: See the system in operation before you make a decision. Kick the tires at someone else's bank.

At many institutions, the strongest barrier against integrated automated documents is tradition. Taking paper for granted is as ingrained in institutional minds as the age rings of a redwood tree. However, there is growing evidence that this predominant view of industrial age thinkers is being chopped down by bankers of the information age.

Islands of Information

In the past, automated document systems that employed imaging technologies have been criticized for shortcomings. Early imaging systems were (and many remain) not well integrated. As a result, banks tend to create "islands of information." Another traditional criticism is that imaging systems required bankers to change their existing policies and structure documents to meet the *needs of the system;* the systems failed to easily adapt to the needs of the bank.

Compared to paper, document images are space hogs of a different species. Document images require tremendous memory storage. Even with data compression, a single document page consumes about 75 to 100 Kbytes of digital storage, equivalent to about 50 text pages. In the mortgage area, for example, adding photographic images or property surveys to a file vastly increases storage requirements.

When these digitized documents and electronic folders travel through departmental or bankwide networks, the resulting traffic jam can be worse than a rush-hour commute. LANs operate at speeds in the 150 Kbytes per second, or two digitized pages per second, which is mighty slow when moving a bulky file. Bankers need to ask if they are trading paper bottlenecks for *electronic* bottlenecks?

Many automated document systems lack the ability to capture key field(s) for automated indexing as the document is created or filled out. Leaving the indexing up to the individuals who create the document will certainly result in lost or misnamed electronic files. So remember, manually indexed automated documents is an oxymoron to avoid.

Serving Customers on Their Coffee Break

The ability to instantly process and grant consumer loans can give a bank the essential edge in an intensely competitive lending market. In 1987, Perpetual Savings Bank adopted CreditRevue, from Credit Management Solutions Inc. (CMSI). This flexible, innovative callup credit processing system provides simultaneous application processing, credit bureau access, and credit scoring and analysis, leading to loan approval before a customer hangs up the phone. It is now called *TeleLoan* at Perpetual Savings Bank.

The system provides lending management at Perpetual Savings Bank with the resources to implement credit policies, achieve better control of risk management, and immediately process customers' loan requests. Customers can conveniently call during their lunch hour, coffee break, or in the evening, and enjoy the privacy that telephone contact allows. After the customer calls 1-800-ALL CASH, an operator gathers and enters the loan application and customer information. The system automatically interfaces with one or more credit bureaus and also integrates credit scoring evaluation according to Perpetual's policies. Based upon the computerized review of customer information, an application can be approved, declined, or forwarded to a credit analyst. TeleLoan enabled the bank to increase loan volume by nearly 50 percent. Of the loan applications received by phone, a decision is reached within 15 minutes for 75 percent of the applicants. Paperwork for approved loans is forwarded to the branch of the customer's choice where the cash is ready and waiting.

James DeFrancesco, president of CMSI, believes the system dovetails with the direction that banks are going. "Beat the clock and you beat the competition; there is no reason why creditworthy customers should have to wait for a credit decision."

FLEETING IMAGES OF CHECK PROCESSING

Image is not a replacement technology. Bankers who just eliminate file cabinets and leave the work process unchanged are missing the real payoffs. Integrated image processing gets at the guts of the banking business. The force and magnitude of change is traumatic. A bank's success in exploiting check image processing will serve to differentiate its products and services from its peers; it can substantially change the nature and structure of a bank's business.

By the late 1980s, breakthroughs in image character recognition married to optical character readers led to successful leading-edge solutions, such as the American Express' image system built by TRW Financial Systems. American Express processes more than 7 million charge slips a day, transmits those images over high-speed communication pipelines, and has achieved tremendous operational savings in addition to customer service benefits. While the American Express image system is clearly a landmark, the pieces of cost-effective, mass-market, integrated-image solutions are only now starting to come together. Most bankers, particularly retail bankers, are not yet moved.

Intimate Bonds

When you consider that current practices of check processing can require a single check to be handled as many as 14 times before return to the originating bank, it is no wonder that check imaging is enticing. A recent Frost & Sullivan report, "The U.S. Market for Image Processing Systems for Banking and Credit Card Applications," summarized the situation: "With 50 billion checks processed each year and more than three percent annual growth, it is clear why even incremental efficiencies can be very worthwhile." How worthwhile? Estimates ranged from a million dollars a year to as high as $30 million. Even though a single entry-level check imaging system can cost two to five million dollars, bankers believe they can recoup their investment within three years.

Strange Bedfellows

Integrated image processing has created some unusual vendor alliances. The Samsons of bank automation—those hardware heavyweights—are chasing Delilah software startups who flaunt their superior expertise. Together these image-mates are creating systems that attack paper-handling processes and bottlenecks with flair, flexibility, and expandability.

In a field where a few years mark a generation, Recognition Equipment Inc.'s (REI) 32-year record of expertise in "information and image recognition" could qualify the company as the great-grandfather in imaging technology. "Partnering is absolutely critical," said Mike Springer, director of product marketing at Dallas-based REI. The company is a leap ahead of most systems in its ability to accurately read handwritten amounts on a check or credit card draft. A function that the majority of bankers feel is essential for an imaging system.

REI and Cincinnati Business Information Systems (CBIS) created ImageBanc, the industry's first image statement product.

In late 1989, Unisys unveiled InfoImage Item Processing. One of the Unisys' collaborators was FileNet Corp., an acknowledged leader in document image processing software utilizing optical disk jukeboxes; Unisys also allied with, and invested in, FileTek for image archiving and mass storage systems. "InfoImage Folder," designed for document image processing, was another technological advance.

> At its introduction, the ImagePlus High-Performance Transaction System (HPST) from IBM was embraced by 26 banks, committed to check-imaging pilot tests. IBM business partners for imaging solutions, which include image titan TRW Financial Systems, could easily fill a bus. Quite a few companies have developed image-enabled document applications to run on IBM mainframes and/or AS/400 platforms.

While scores of big banks are still flirting with imaging, the $3.5 billion asset First Interstate Bank of Washington is a veteran. Senior vice president Vern Canfield started exploring check image statements in 1981, partly as a method to combat rising postage costs. "When Photo Check was launched in 1984, recalls Canfield, "43 percent selected the product, after two years it became the choice for 57 percent." In addition to satisfying the bank's customers, Canfield satisfied his CEO by slashing postage costs by more than $200,000 a year.

In March 1990, First Interstate installed its second-generation image system developed by REI and CBIS. "The new system provided better quality images, improved image compression and used workstations to incorporate imaging throughout the check-processing cycle rather than only at the back end," explained Canfield.

CBIS is already extending the boundaries of image statements with a new product called *DocuBanc*, which enables bankers to customize customer statements and notices by selectively adding marketing messages, or by creating large-print formats for senior citizens, or statements in Spanish for Spanish-speaking consumers."

Pittsburgh-based Mellon Bank pioneered imaging applications in many areas, and was one of six banks that started plotting a check-imaging solution with IBM in late 1986. Mellon senior vice president Gilbert Arbuckle shared his perspectives on imaging with bankers at a recent ABA meeting. "The full impact of imaging won't appear until the last half of the decade; however, the technology can immediately revolutionize how banks process checks," believes Arbuckle. Mellon started by incorporating imaging in front-end functions, such as encoding and reject processing.

Savings Attributed to Imaging

- Transaction volume per employee increases by 25 to 40 percent
- Staff reductions of 20 to 30 percent
- Floor space reductions (for paper storage) of up to 50 percent
- Transaction processing time cut by 50 percent
- Cost reduction of 30 percent, excluding the cost of the imaging system

PAYOFFS AND PITFALLS

The road to imaging is not as carefree as some bankers might think. Every banker has some cautions to share. Retraining staff is a major endeavor because employees need new skill sets. "Staff selection, workflow management, and area supervision are more critical because of the processing interdependencies," explained a banker. The dark side of booming productivity is that, since processing per employee can double to 2,500 items a day, absenteeism can set a bank's operations back faster than ever before.

At Mellon Bank, "document design or redesign emerged as a key factor for success," said Arbuckle. Standardizing deposit tickets, internal credit/debit memos, and even teller validation stamping is no easy task, not to mention coping with the popular scenic check." Those furry animals and pictures of ships that bump into check amount boxes can wreck havoc in imaging. Red ink and pencil-written checks are also problems.

Taking the Plunge

Hugh Ryan a partner with Andersen Consulting in Chicago, identified trust, cash management, and customer services as prime candidate departments for document imaging, or "case" image processing in Ryan's vernacular. "Image case processing is particularly well-suited for decentralized functions that require heavy data/information retrieval," notes Ryan. "For example, a mortgage file with 50 to 130 pages can be image-processed in parallel," Ryan stated, "as opposed to standard paper-based, linear processing when a physical file must be routed," explains Ryan. Better utilization of human resources and improvements in customer service are two of Ryan's image by-products.

Citibank's credit card inquiry operation in Sioux Falls, South Dakota installed 70 IBM ImagePlus workstations to deal with more than 8,000 customer letters a day. "Productivity is up by 20 to 25 percent," said John Young, Citibank vice president and director of customer services.

For Better or Worse

On the surface, transaction image systems seem to share the same approach, the mission is to "marry traditional high-speed reader/ sorters with scanners and OCR systems and perfect a data/image database," explained REI's Springer.

Bankers have confirmed suppliers claims of the quantum leaps in staff productivity. The cost savings from eliminating operator positions average from 30 percent to better than 50 percent depending on the existing technology base. Bankers also envision efficiencies in being able to centralize processing and check image archiving, and anticipate opportunities for new fee-based, value-added services. Future advances, such as the integration of expert systems for check balancing functions, reject repair and other tasks will keep imaging a hotbed of activity for many years to come.

Apart from the top 250 financial institutions, most banks are not going to benefit immediately from high-volume, high-speed image transaction systems. The costs to ante up in check or credit card image-processing are still too high for the masses. However, targeted, low-volume, niche applications certainly make sense for the uninitiated. In the words of Andersen Consulting's Ryan, "A pilot is worth 10,000 discussions."

Look for innovative, low risk-high reward opportunities. Exploit imaging to make faster decisions. Any bank could test imaging in a lending situation by "breaking down an auto or consumer loan application into key parts and saving costs by using automated tools to reach a decision earlier in the review using a 'limited chunk' of data," suggested REI's Springer.

Backfile conversion is one of the most difficult and challenging decisions in incorporating imaging into an existing application. How much "backfill" is necessary, and how long does it take? Well, first consider the cost factor—backfile conversion can easily reach $200,000, roughly equivalent to the cost of a departmental image system.

Despite the drawbacks and costs, there is no question that imaging has the potential to profoundly transform retail banking. Some compare imaging to the invention of the printing press and the typewriter. Moving closer to the banker's domain, one banker stated "The impact that image-processing will have on the banking industry will be as great, if not greater, than the impact that magnetic ink character recognition (MICR) technology had 25 years ago." And while some analysts claim that imaging is a greater breakthrough than PCs or local area networking in the 1980s, aspects of the integrated imaging revolution were spawned in these very advances.

Both large-scale and departmental system developers are adopting the same "rules of the game":

- **Standards**   In many ways, IBM is setting the standard for multi-platform systems. This should come as no surprise to retail bankers. The ImagePlus system operates in the same or similar manner across all hardware platforms from mainframe to AS/400 to PS/2. Most vendors are migrating to accepted computer industry networking and operating system standards. This will preserve the bank's investments and facilitate "integrated image processing."
- **Modularity**   This feature enables bankers to pursue an "evolutionary" approach to incorporating imaging in steps as well as adding enhancements and new versions of image systems as they reach the market.
- **Multivendor Solutions**   Not only do standards promote multi-vendor solutions but supplier alliances give bankers less customization compared to data processing 20 years ago.
- **Lower Costs**   The cost of document imaging is falling rapidly. Although it remains beyond the grasp of small banks it will continue to be a viable cost-effective investment for medium-sized financial institutions.

Rules to Live By

The cardinal rules for new image product development, either departmental automated document systems or product-based programs, such as imaged check statements, include the following:

- Seizing new opportunities, and quickly bringing new or hybrid products to market
- Targeting customers or customer segments for new products

- Smart marketing, advertising, and promotion at product introduction to capture customer interest
- Pricing new products and services for profitability
- Keeping customer convenience and quality customer service foremost in the new product formula
- Incorporating flexibility and simplicity into new products so they are easy to understand and easy to sell, with benefits that can be tailored to a individual customer needs
- The "fit" into the overall product line; products building upon other successful products and complementing the bank's business growth strategies
- Taking advantage of alliances with suppliers to incorporate their experience and expertise, and sharing the costs of developments

If bankers are to achieve the rewards of integrated imaging processing, they must accept and build upon the technologies of the past. They must seize the opportunities to migrate existing technologies to imaging platforms and solutions and incorporate other conventional procedures and/or technologies wherever practical. It is more than merely recognizing or appreciating the heredity of bank automation.

In the final analysis, it is not an imaging issue at all. It is an *information processing* issue. Perhaps the most important question to pose is: Do you really need to divorce yourself from today's tried and true information systems to behold the image of the future?

7

Marketing Systems and Strategies

The bank marketing master and the chess master are cut from the same cloth. Both are astute students of the games they play, constantly learning and refining their skills. They study their opponents' moves, and take advantage of every blunder. As in chess, retail bank marketing players must also make sacrifices during their game—these can be staff cuts, budget constraints, canceled campaigns, and organizational politics. They must even adjust their strategies for the vagaries of the economy and the financial industry at large.

THE MARKETER'S MISSION

Many bank CEOs are wary of bank marketing managers with their razzle-dazzle product promotions, market segmentation jargon, and ever-rising budget requirements. In response to this scrutiny, the marketer must maneuver many pieces to effectively plan and launch campaigns, track results, coordinate with the branch sales staff, build market share and revenues and optimize customer/product profitability. All the while, the marketer remains focused on the goal—the customer is king.

Cross-selling existing customers certainly is an important component of the marketing endeavor; many bankers believe it is easier and more cost-effective to sell new accounts to known, old-standby customers. New-customer acquisition can be expensive. However, rather than focusing on the expense of new-account recruitment, retail bankers need to look at the potential relationship and life-cycle value of new customers to gain a truer picture of a new customer's net worth to the bank. At the very least, banks need to replace the five to eight percent of "lost" households—customers who move outside the bank's territory or just relocate their accounts to other institutions with perceived greener pastures, slicker services, or more successful marketing messages.

In the old days, marketing managers were bit players in the business of retail banking. There was quite a bit of instinctive, seat-of-the-pants decision-making. Mass marketing was the norm. Media were limited to customer brochures, statement stuffers, branch "signage," and the typical CD or mortgage rate ads in the local newspaper.

Today, the top marketing executives are respected and even revered by their CEOs and colleagues. They use revolutionary technology to take bold steps in market planning and campaigns. In the battle against the competition for market share, the bank marketing master is a field general who relies on extensive customer data, sophisticated statistics, and colorful maps and charts. A vast arsenal of high-tech, information-rich weapons are used to wage the good fight and marketing strategies learned and borrowed from other industries are skillfully deployed.

Lest anyone think that every other bank is miles ahead in marketing capabilities, a 1989 study by the Bank Marketing Association and Andersen Consulting is worth examining. Bankers' self-rank in marketing prowess was at the bottom of the barrel, barely edging out retail boutiques. Bankers viewed credit card, insurance, and brokerage companies as more skilled marketers. These companies are the nonbanks that are direct competitors for customers' dollars. Survey participants realized that to remain competitive and profitable in a deregulated environment, banks must beef up their marketing muscle.

Perhaps the situation has changed, but a complete marketing transformation does not happen in a flash. Consider the challenges and the situation in more detail. In what may be termed the *three strikes* against bankers—3 in 5 banks lack relationship marketing systems for direct mail, only 3 in 20 use telemarketing technology, and a mere 3 in 50 can effectively track product promotions. Half the bankers surveyed confessed to an inability to integrate customer information for cross-selling.

RESEARCH AND PLANNING

Quest for Knowledge

The best place to begin is by asking a few hard questions to define the bank's strengths, weaknesses, and market position. The opening move in the bank marketing game is *market research*, which is more of an ongoing process than an event. It requires collecting and analyzing a wide variety of information to define the bank's existing market share, the best customer prospects, and the right mix of marketing media to find, contact, and acquire new customers or capitalize on expanding markets. Parts of the data reside within the bank's information systems, other pieces can be bought on the open market.

In the hands of an innovative banker, information can turn marginal customers into profitable ones. Cross-selling products and services to customers is greatly facilitated with the right tools. Marketing systems support "bank retailing" in local, regional, and bankwide campaigns.

Sizing Up the Competition

One essential step in market research is calculating the total retail banking market, your bank's share, and "trends" in market expansion or erosion. How easy is it to identify and define your opponents and their weaknesses?

Perpetual Savings Bank uses COMPASS, an integrated desktop marketing system from Claritas, to get a clear reading on market share. "For example," explains a Perpetual marketer, "I can view an onscreen map of Fairfax county, Virginia, locate my branches and all of my competitor's branches and see the distribution of customers and penetration, by product, in a matter of minutes."

Combining COMPASS with Claritas reporting, the marketing staff can evaluate the bank's performance and market share compared to other banks and nonbanks in the area or to all institutions of the same asset-size. Standard reports rank competitive institutions according to any selected criteria. Quarterly shifts in market share are noted at the 90 or 95 percent confidence level. Years ago such an exercise would take a marketing manager days or weeks, so it competitive analysis at the product level was often skipped. Since COMPASS is interactive, you can ask any number of questions and explore "what-if" scenarios and get immediate results in customer list, graph, or map form.

BankSource, the Bank Analysis and Forecasting System from Ferguson & Co. of Irving, Texas, is a PC-based interactive marketing and management tool, which provides instantaneous access to detailed current as well as three-year financial histories on all FDIC-insured commercial banks. The financial database, supplied on optical disks, is updated quarterly. According to president and company founder, William Ferguson, "With BankSource, it becomes much easier to track institutional, peer group or industry trends, monitor expense levels, guide pricing policies, and evaluate competitive institutions."

The peer group analysis feature enables business planning officers at Buffalo-based, superregional Marine Midland Bank to perform insightful comparisons with key competitors. "We have been doing peer group studies for a long while," explained a Marine Midland banker, "with BankSource it is much faster, and we can get greater depth of analysis. We pour the data into Lotus 1-2-3 for spreadsheet reports, forecasts, and presentations."

Alternatively, banks can tap into data in The Financial Registry database from Donnelly Marketing Information Services. Use of these data facilitates market assessment, competitive identification, and calculation of market share. Donnelly's data include commercial and savings banks, savings and loans, and credit unions.

A number of bank marketers rely on market penetration studies, using decision support tools from Urban Science Applications, Inc. (USAI). Graphic displays and reports show the distribution of bank and branch performance compared to marketplace potential as well as a markets' expansion and contraction over time. USAI studies can be used to evaluate current or past performance as well as to forecast and plan future strategies. USAI also offers GAIN, a PC-based decision support system for market and distribution analysis. It combines customer and market profiles with sophisticated modeling techniques. Using this system, a bank can assess branch performance, choose the best location for new branches based on competition, convenience, and market revenue potential.

In a field where nothing is fixed, one thing can be said with certainty. Marketing masters are not afraid of statistics. They are not intimidated by numbers. Beware of the pseudomasters who rely on anecdotes, industry gossip, and the mass media for marketing planning and decision support. Marketing masters do not take a shortcut around the solid base of statistics about customers and competitors.

MARKETING CIFs

Moves for Competitive Advantage

A trademark of marketing masters is their use of marketing customer information files (MCIFs) as tracking and support systems. Tracking systems are essential to deal with the cost benefit elements. Industry surveys indicate that, by simply tracking sales activity and prospective customer contact information, a bank can increase its sales by 20 percent or more. Recently, microcomputer-based marketing CIFs have attracted much attention. In general, they require relatively low dollar investment, link into the bank's existing mainframe or minibased online CIF, and can be deployed to pursue a database marketing program for cross-selling. CIF data is commonly downloaded to MCIFs on a quarterly or monthly basis.

Customer Development Corporation knows a thing or two about customers. They create, match, research and update financial files totaling 70 million accounts every month. Their PC-based Marketing File Access System (MFAS) can be used to get answers to questions like: "How many households with aggregate balances of $50K plus in savings products have checking accounts?" or "What is the risk of adding a service charge to low balance savings accounts?"

As an option with Customer Development Corporation's integrated selling systems, banks can choose the PC-based Marketing File Access System (MFAS). This system allows a bank to produce and print a variety of reports on any subset of the customer files. For example, the "Geopen Report" can show household penetration listed by census tract for any or all branches. Other data for analysis can include median household income, equity value of owner-occupied structures, current housing value, and the age of the current mortgage. Armed with such information, marketing masters plan home equity programs that can be coordinated at the local branch level.

Genesis, a desktop MCIF system from CDC can generate cross-sell reports on a million customer accounts in less than two minutes.The grahics-capable system provides 138 separate fields for customer data; it interfaces with CDC's database management and planning services.

Another PC-based MCIF that retail bankers may want to examine is MicroMarketer, from Okra Marketing Corporation. Features and enhancements of MicroMarketer include product repricing analysis, automated letter generation and mail merge, and a separate profitability module to analyze product profitability and distribution. OKRA also provides a local area network system of its TotalMarketer MCIF system intended for big banks.

Since 1979, Security Pacific Bank has relied on a marketing customer information system called CIS from Harte-Hanks Data Technologies. CIS formats household customer data for a variety of marketing applications; it complements a bank's in-house data with census information, purchased lists, or other demographic databases. A micro-computer version, P/CIS, is also available.

Security Pacific was a development and test site for CIS/Direct. This database management system enables banks to better plan, target, and track direct marketing programs including telemarketing, direct mail, and personal selling. An assistant vice president and manager of direct response at Security Pacific, claimed "CIS/Direct can quickly and reliably show us the results of our promotions and help us see where we can enhance the way we communicate with our customers." In addition, CIS/Direct provides data on response, revenue generated, direct marketing costs, and household relationship changes.

Nearly half of the nation's top financial institutions use marketing customer information systems from Harte-Hanks Data Technologies. Systems include custom databases, direct marketing tools, and desktop marketing systems. In 1989, Harte-Hanks unveiled CIS/Direct, which automates and manages all forms of direct response marketing from telemarketing and direct mail to personal selling and other direct customer communications. One benefit of this MCIF module is the ability to perform precision customer profiling at the officer level by product and/or by transaction activity.

The Peoples MCIF

James Polito is vice president and director of market planning and research at the **Peoples Savings Bank** based in Bridgeport, Connecticut. This state bank operates 72 branches, holds $6 billion assets, and serves customers with 1.4 million accounts. Polito recalled, "Five years ago, Peoples could not find out about our own customers very easily." Specialized reports were very time-consuming. At the same time, the already heated competition in mortgage lending was reaching the boiling point with 650 companies actively pursuing home and office buyers/builders in the state.

Peoples appointed a task force to assess the bank's needs and set a course to evaluate, select, and implement a new marketing CIF system. The team included members from data processing, marketing, product marketing, a regional office representative, and finance. "Top management," Polito stated, "was the key silent partner."

Included in the list of needs were current customer total relationship (accounts, products used, and balance), product profiles, householding, sales results tracking, geographic market penetration and potential, and branch, customer, and product profitability. The process has been long and deliberate. Along the way, task force members questioned themselves to determine what an MCIF can and cannot do. For example, the MCIF cannot be used to determine the bank's market share or competitive financial firms used by customers, or to assess the bank customer's product purchase intentions.

One thing is certain. Peoples is on the move. They have acquired or merged with six banks in the last nine years. And according to Polito, they intend to use their MCIF as a weapon to "aggressively compete against Bank of Boston, BayBanks, and others" on the battleground of banking.

An MCIF adds the "meat" of customer psychographics and lifestyle profiling to a skin and bones, transaction accounting CIF. It gives bankers something to sharpen their marketing tools for planning purposes, and provides the sales staff with something to sink their teeth into during cross-sell encounters.

PC-based MCIFs, such as the PROFILE Marketing workstation from Management Science Associates, Inc. include complete customer account information: date of birth, phone numbers, date of first service, householding, geocoding, and standard account balance and activity data. MCIFs can generate cross-sell ratio reports and assist the bank's marketing department in targeting baby boomers for new products and services. PROFILE can even provide a database of baby boomers who have left the bank to attempt reestablishing relationships before lost baby boomers become forgotten.

One Bank U.S.

Market research at **Citibank** is taking a new turn. The existing main marketing system, dubbed BRIMS—Banking Relationship Information Management System—had been created to meet the needs of the New York customer base. Now with its national leadership position in bankcards and mortgages, Citibank is consolidating customer information nationwide. The new system, in the final stages of in-house development is code-named ONUS—One Bank U.S. It is expected to be operational by the end of 1992.

The system is expected to process complex requests for information on "micro markets," right down to the individual household level. The relational database can be queried in countless ways, such as: "Provide a list of households with $50,000 or more in annual income, that write more than 25 checks per month with an average monthly checking balance of $3,000 who do not own a Citibank bankcard."

Customers may have no hiding place from ONUS, and non-Citibankers may have no shelter from the direct marketing storm.

Bankers who have mastered the fundamentals of a MCIF system soon learn that they need to know more details about their customers' financial habits and needs. The importance of accurately targeting the bank's marketing messages for "customer subgroups." Is often another revelation. And to complete the marketing triangle, bankers also need high-tech tools to analyze product promotion results.

DATABASE MARKETING

Database marketing, sometimes referred to as integrated marketing, is a term that marketers toss about freely when sermonizing on bank marketing strategies and goals. In essence, database marketing is plotting and directing campaigns based on countless, related pieces of data about customers and their financial habits and needs. A common industry problem is that bank databases are often built around the institution's needs rather than customers' needs. While certain retail bankers struggle to sell *products*, marketing masters are busy selling *customers*.

Databases can be searched, sorted, and segmented into targeted customer groups, often coded according to standard profiles. Segmentation enables marketers to make sound assumptions about prospective customers by knowing how a similar *known* group of customers behave financially. Why and when do they buy and use financial products as they do? What attracts these customers to a particular institution or product?

Market segmentation typically encompasses three primary elements:

- Geographic data, such as population and census tract information
- Demographics, including the age, occupation, education, income, marital status, and household composition
- Psychographics research, which uncovers golden nuggets of information about customers' spending and saving habits, lifestyles, and financial behavior patterns

Slick customer segmentation is how the retail bank marketing maximizes response in relation to expense.

Chase Manhattan Bank has designed and constructed a "rich" database to cross-market products to the wealthy and affluent. Although these upper-echelon markets comprise only 8.7 percent of all households, they account for 58 percent of the financial assets held by individuals. And, according to a Chase spokesperson, "these upper crusts are growing faster than the market overall. The Chase database marketing center is the information hub or 'relationship manager' for the affluent market."

The Chase database is a melting pot of geodemographic segmentation profiles, the bank's own customer records and product usage data, and other pertinent information. For geodemographic data, Chase uses a segmentation system from Claritas Corporation, a leading provider of target marketing data. Claritas's P$YCLE classifies every neighborhood in the United States according to its socioeconomic characteristics. Chase focuses on those segments that describe key characteristics of the wealthy and affluent, particularly their income-producing assets. Armed with this inside strategic information, the bank develops campaigns and plans according to customers' needs and timing those needs.

Complete understanding of a customer's needs is an elusive goal, like trying to catch a fly with chopsticks. Advances in data collection and database technology help the masters target smaller segments and look more closely at opportunities at the local and micro, or neighborhood, level.

Claritas excels in the quality of local market data. At the neighborhood and "zip cluster" level, database linkages—correlations of key information—become particularly valuable and fundamentally more reliable. Focusing on smaller geographic areas, like branch neighborhoods, requires more, not less, information and analysis.

American Savings Bank, competes against Chase and other institutions in the highly heterogeneous New York metropolitan area. The market research department at American Savings Bank, relies heavily on Equifax Marketing Decision Systems' data to evaluate market opportunities. With VISION, Equifax's market segmentation facility, the bank can test and target direct mail to a desirable audience of noncustomers. A bank spokesperson recalled, "A student loan mailing to a randomly selected list of high-school seniors, pulled a three percent response. A second mailing, to a group culled from VISION-coded customers with a 'propensity to purchase student loans,' generated a response of nearly seven percent." American Savings' MCIF incorporates VISION segmentation codes and provides the springboard to learn more about the lifestyles of customers and their evolving relationships with the thrift. American Savings Bank also uses the information to compare current customers against VISION national trends and norms.

Another resource to assess the sales potential of a territory or neighborhood is the PC-based FinancialPac from Equifax Marketing Decision Systems. Bankers can search and sort a wealth of demographic data plus FDIC information and the SRI financial consumer demand database, which includes estimates of the amount of money households have to spend on 20 different financial services and products.

Premier Bancorp, a market leader and a bank skilled in market research, is based in Baton Rouge, Louisiana. Premier's marketing and strategic planning staff use "lots of different information sources about the bank's customers and other bank's customers, and relies heavily on VISION codes," according to a bank spokesperson. Premier's marketing director believes "birds of a feather flock together." As a result, he looks at "customers who live in (VISION-coded) 'Carports and Kids' neighborhoods to see what types of bank products they use in general and what particular products they have a propensity for. For example, if the bank wants to reach middle-class town residents in a part of Louisiana, we can zero in on three segments of the VISION database—'Mainstreet USA', 'Town and Country', and 'Tom Sawyerville' to compile a suitable list." Based on nationwide trends and our own customer information, we already have a fairly descriptive profile of these customers' financial needs and interests. To capture new customers we may send a direct mail package offering a checking account with no fees for the first year as an incentive to leave their present bank and join us." The success in using the VISION database has confirmed Premier bankers' belief that an address is the key ingredient in knowing quite a bit about a prospect.

On the basis on the analysis, Premier has developed cross-selling campaigns and promotions for car loans, mortgages, and bank cards. The bank also uses telemarketing to sell such products as tax-deferred annuities; incentives bait targeted noncustomers. "Since checking is the most important core product," said Premier's spokesperson, "we offer free checking accounts for one year to get prospective customers to switch."

Different criteria rise to the forefront as bank marketers define and redefine target segments. Customers needs change, market opportunities shift, and new products must be created to fill in the gaps. New strategies and techniques to effectively reach customers are also emerging at retail banks across the country.

DIRECT CONTACT AND TELEMARKETING

To the Customer's Castle

Direct marketing is the vehicle of choice by bank marketing masters surveyed. Direct marketing puts your message in front of the customer at home. You are not fighting for attention against other newspaper advertisers. And you exert the most control to customize your message for the targeted audience, and track customer response.

Since the mid-1980s, marketers at Midlantic Bank, based in Edison, New Jersey, have been using Claritas PRIZM segments to guide direct marketing campaigns and media buys according to Midlantic's senior vice president of marketing. "The bank has always enjoyed a strong market share of the upscale customer; we look closely at all S1, 2, 3, and 4 (S codes stand for *Suburban* neighborhoods) households in our areas—New Jersey, eastern Pennsylvania, and upstate New York." The S codes correspond to 11 of Claritas' 40 lifestyle/neighborhood clusters, that are known by such nicknames as "Money & Brains", "Levittown, U.S.A." and "Blue-Chip Blues." See Figure 7–1.

Midlantic has found direct mail works best for local marketing and for cross-selling new customers. A bank spokesperson explained, "Direct mail works particularly well for home equity loan products, high-yield savings accounts, and other investments." Midlantic generates a list by PRIZM codes where those codes are dominant in zip clusters where we have branches. Midlantic's "Hungary Savers Fund" has been an extremely effective and successful product. The accounts, with $25K or $50K minimums, are variable rate instruments tied to the the Donahue money market averages.

Reach Out and Touch Your Customers

More banks are calling upon telemarketing as they plot their marketing strategies. This is an area where high-tech meets high-touch. Where professional, trained salespeople armed with scripts make a targeted, outbound, Touch-Tone connection with customers. And where computer technology supports every encounter. For those bankers who think it may be too early to use telemarketing as part of the bank's sales operation, you may want to rethink your assumptions.

For high-volume, outbound telemarketing, some banks have linked integrated voice/data terminals to their CIFs. Using a computerized

P · R · I · Z · M

Market Segmentation & Targeting by Neighborhood Life-Style Clusters

THE 40 CLUSTER SYSTEM

THE FORTY LIFE-STYLE CLUSTERS

PERCENT 1985 U.S. HOUSEHOLDS

Nicknames				One-Liners							Black-Cluster Model Groups / Clusters	Tract-Cluster Model Groups / Clusters	ZIP-Cluster Model Groups / Clusters
Blue Blood Estates	DEN5	SUBS	DOM	FAM	4/3	CG	WC	SU	O 1			1.12 / 0.84	/ 0.84	/ 0.64
Money & Brains	DEN7	SUBS	DOM	FAM	4/5	CG	WC	SU	O 2			0.94 / 0.99	/ 0.99	/ 1.14
Furs & Station Wagons	DEN5	SUBS	DOM	FAM	3/4	CG	WC	SU	O 3			3.16 / 2.67	4.60 / 2.67	4.21 / 2.44
Pools & Patios	DEN6	SUBS	DOM	MIX	3/4	CG	WC	SU	O 5			3.41 / 3.66	/ 3.66	/ 3.28
Two More Rungs	DEN6	SUBS	MIX	FS	3/5	CG	WC	SU	O 6			0.74 / 0.85	7.13 / 0.85	7.33 / 1.03
Young Influentials	DEN7	SUBS	DOM	FS	1/2	CG	WC	MU	O 7			2.85 / 2.62	/ 2.62	/ 3.02
Young Suburbia	DEN5	SUBS	DOM	FAM	3/2	CG	WC	SU	O 8			5.33 / 5.45	11.59 / 5.45	10.53 / 5.64
Blue-Chip Blues	DEN5	SUBS	DOM	FAM	4/2	CG	WC	SU	O10			6.00 / 6.13	/ 6.13	/ 5.19
Urban Gold Coast	DEN9	CITY	MIX	SGL	2/6	HS	WC	MU	O 4			0.47 / 0.49	/ 0.49	/ 0.45
Bohemian Mix	DEN9	CITY	MIX	SGL	3/4	HS	WC	MU	O11			1.14 / 1.16	/ 1.16	/ 0.81
Black Enterprise	DEN7	SUBS	DOM	FAM	3/4	SC	WC	29	O14			0.76 / 0.75	7.52 / 0.75	7.25 / 1.21
New Beginnings	DEN7	CITY	MIX	FS	2/1	SC	WC	MU	O15			4.30 / 5.12	/ 5.12	/ 4.77
God's Country	DEN2	TOWN	DOM	FAM	3/2	CG	WC	SU	O 9			2.70 / 2.37	/ 2.37	/ 2.97
New Homesteaders	DEN3	TOWN	DOM	FAM	4/5	SC	WC	SU	O17			4.15 / 4.76	8.53 / 4.76	10.23 / 5.08
Towns & Gowns	DEN3	TOWN	DOM	SGL	1/2	SC	WC	SU	O19			1.17 / 1.39	/ 1.39	/ 2.18
Levittown, U.S.A.	DEN6	SUBS	DOM	CPL	5/6	HS	SC	SU	O12			3.05 / 3.29	/ 3.29	/ 4.51
Gray Power	DEN5	SUBS	DOM	CPL	5/6	SC	WC	MU	O13			2.50 / 2.04	6.71 / 2.04	7.84 / 2.28
Rank & File	DEN6	SUBS	MIX	CPL	2/9	BC	WC	29	O20			1.42 / 1.37	/ 1.37	/ 1.07
Blue-Collar Nursery	DEN2	CITY	DOM	FAM	3/2	HS	BC	SU	O16			2.24 / 2.41	/ 2.41	/ 1.70
Middle America	DEN4	TOWN	DOM	FAM	4/5	HS	BC	SU	O21			3.19 / 3.54	7.98 / 3.54	9.01 / 4.76
Coalburg & Corntown	DEN2	TOWN	DOM	SGL	6/3	HS	BC	SU	O23			1.96 / 2.02	/ 2.02	/ 2.55
New Melting Pot	DEN9	CITY	MIX	FS	6/5	HS	WC	MU	O18			0.91 / 0.95	/ 0.95	/ 1.33
Old Yankee Rows	DEN7	CITY	MIX	FS	6/5	HS	BC	29	O22			1.60 / 1.84	7.96 / 1.84	/ 1.80
Emergent Minorities	DEN7	CITY	MIX	FAM	6/3	HS	BW	SU	O28			1.73 / 1.78	/ 1.78	/ 2.07
Single City Blues	DEN8	CITY	MIX	SGL	2/9	BC	WC	MU				3.34 / 2.75	7.58 / 2.75	7.27 / 2.08
Shotguns & Pickups	DEN1	FARM	DOM	FAM	3/4	HS	BF	BW	O06			1.87 / 1.84	/ 1.84	/ 2.53
Agri-Business	DEN1	FARM	DOM	FAM	4/3	EX	BF	BW	O08			2.13 / 2.62	5.69 / 2.62	6.24 / 4.26
Grain Belt	DEN0	FARM	DOM	FAM	6/5	HS	BF	SU	O33			1.27 / 1.23	/ 1.23	/ 1.43
Golden Ponds	DEN3	TOWN	DOM	CPL	3/4	SC	BW	SU	O25			5.24 / 5.03	/ 5.03	/ 3.05
Mines & Mills	DEN3	TOWN	DOM	FAM	5/4	HS	BC	SU	O29			2.84 / 2.60	13.13 / 2.60	/ 1.85
Norma Rae-Ville	DEN3	TOWN	MIX	FAM	1/4	SH	BC	SU	O31			2.32 / 2.75	/ 2.75	9.51 / 2.95
Smalltown Downtown	DEN6	TOWN	DOM	FS	6/1	HS	BW	29	O32			2.46 / 2.76	/ 2.76	/ 1.95
Back-Country Folks	DEN1	TOWN	DOM	FAM	6/3	SH	BC	SU	O30			3.42 / 3.16	/ 3.16	/ 4.29
Share Croppers	DEN1	TOWN	MIX	FAM	6/5	GS	BF	SU	O35			4.00 / 3.78	9.06 / 3.78	/ 3.65
Tobacco Roads	DEN0	TOWN	DOM	FS	1/4	GS	BF	29	O38			1.22 / 0.98	/ 0.98	9.52 / 0.96
Hard Scrabble	DEN0	FARM	MIX	FAM	6/5	GS	BF	SU	O39			1.51 / 1.05	/ 1.05	/ 1.03
Heavy Industry	DEN7	CITY	MIX	FS	6/5	SH	BC	29	O04			2.75 / 2.52	/ 2.52	/ 1.95
Downtown Dixie-Style	DEN8	CITY	DOM	SGL	1/2	GS	SS	BS	O07			3.39 / 3.51	10.65 / 3.51	10.85 / 2.30
Hispanic Mix	DEN9	CITY	DOM	SGL	1/5	SH	BS	29	O27			1.88 / 1.94	/ 1.94	/ 1.52
Public Assistance	DEN8	CITY	DOM	SS	1/6	GS	BS	SU	O40			3.12 / 2.57	/ 2.57	9.07 / 2.30
Total U.S.											100.00 / 100.00	100.00 / 100.00	100.00 / 100.00

Figure 7-1. Market segmentation and targeting by neighborhood lifestyle clusters.

autodial system, banks can automatically dial customer phone numbers from one or more CIFs to conduct a targeted marketing campaign. When a customer answers, the workstation retrieves the customer file and delivers it to the operator's screen. The same workstation can be used for inbound customer service calls. Telemarketing software tracks and analyzes leads and sales, and generates reports on personal productivity and cross selling. These systems can also calculate earned commissions.

First Interstate Bank of California generated more than $100 million in new business in one year as a result of telemarketing. The bank focused on three primary outbound strategies: follow-up of new accounts, capturing the rollover revenues of maturing CDs, and contacting depositors who look like good loan prospects.

Due to technological advances in telemarketing systems and the voice/data terminals, a number of other bank marketers are testing inbound and outbound telemarketing for everything from home equity loans, to IRAs, savings investments, credit cards, and other financial products.

The telemarketing department at Perpetual Savings Bank has been selling and closing sales with customers since 1985. A Perpetual spokesperson elaborated "We'll generate a list of new customers like suburban 'Young Influentials,' the nickname for another Claritas market segment. Based on their profile I know that new 'Young Influential' checking account customers have a high propensity to purchase other bank products such as a line of credit or money market savings account. I know who they are and I want more of them." Perpetual has used outbound telemarketing and direct mail with 800 number response options to effectively cross-sell and efficiently capture new customers. Perpetual has also explored the medium of television, running ads based on the PRIZM-coded Neilson and Arbitron viewer ratings.

Hits and Misses

Who is winning in the high-tech bank marketing game? Ultimately, the customer is the winner. The customer receives better service, products better suited to their particular needs and more "customized" attention. If customers are satisfied you know you've done the job right. Getting a new customer is only half the battle, retaining them is the other half.

Where are the weak links in a technologically enriched marketing strategy, the pitfalls that bank marketing champions look to avoid? One problem in the trend to micromarketing is always "looking through the big end of the telescope." Sometimes marketers are so concerned about the details that they overlook the big picture, like a big drop or rise in interest rates, for example.

Following-up on leads is still an area where retail banks are weakest. In extreme cases, some bankers confess that it can take as long as six months to act on leads. New customer prospects are highly a perishable commodity. The time to sell or close a sale is short. You already know that the customer is shopping," a veteran bank marketer explains, "if you don't move quickly they will land somewhere else." Get fresh leads out to sales people in the telemarketing trenches and in the branches.

One industry consultant described the missing pieces as "time and event processing." There are precise situations and events that pinpoint a customer's "propensity to buy" or the likelihood of a need. These habits, trends, and events in product usage—data that is often buried in the CIF—are the strongest messages that tend to elude nearly all bankers. It is much better information than any demographics a bank can buy. Event response is a variation of following-up but it is triggered in an intuitive manner. And as with leads, the likelihood of purchase diminishes as the time period lengthens after the key event.

Many bankers fail to see the difference and the *sequence* of marketing and sales. Remember selling is a short-term score. Marketing is a preselling and postselling process. Bankers think they need a sales culture, but they actually need a marketing culture. Marketer Ted Levitt offers this lesson: "Marketing focuses on the needs of the customer and develops products and services to meet ongoing needs and generate new demands for products and services. In contrast, selling focuses on the needs of the seller and getting product off the shelf." A bank must be sales-capable first, otherwise it's like running an expensive car without an engine—you will have something that looks good, but it won't take you anywhere. Lots of banks seem to be sales-oriented, but when you look closely they are not there.

Lastly, don't lose sight of the customer. It is easy to start relating to customers by their alleged labels, psychographics, and "propensities" in the effort to categorize and quantify customer's financial habits and behaviors. Don't forget that you are dealing with real people, not just pieces on the game board of retail banking.

8

Sales and Staff Performance

SALES CULTURE SHOCK

A retail bank product, be it a checking account or a mortgage, is a consumer commodity. Like any other commodity, it has perceived value to the customer, and it can be positioned in the marketplace. As a product, it has a character, an identity, and a track record of sales.

The mission for retail bankers is to take a clear "retailing" orientation in defining, packaging, promoting, and selling bank products to current and prospective customers. The other prerequisite for this new-age bank retailing is infusing the bank's infrastructure with a sales-driven orientation.

The handwriting spelling out the banker's new role has been on the wall for quite some time. Twenty-five years ago, A. M. Porat and J. A. Vaughan wrote in an article on "Branch Management and Computers" in *Banking Magazine* that

> The retail bank concept with all the new innovations derived from (electronic data processing) has changed the bank manager's function into that of a sales manager. Responsibilities for clean operations and sound lending practices are second to the sales goal necessary to reach satisfactory quotas. Clerical staff has become a selling staff, and sales emphasis has required a complete change in learning and training practices.

Establishing a sales culture runs deep into the core of an organization. Cultural change involves the attitudes, habits and behaviors of the bank as an institution as well as of its people. Evolving a true sales culture in a bank takes time. One banker interviewed estimated that it requires three to five years of directed, consistent effort. A memo or a meeting will not a culture make.

Organizational Imperatives

There is no mystery in remaking the organization, to recasting its mission and image. Begin by sketching the overall retail banking strategy: goals, objectives, action plans, tactics. Evaluate the existing structure, including operations, staffing, support systems, and procedures, as well as the dominant business and banking trends. Then come the soul-searching questions: What is the real nature of our business? What should the nature of our business become? What is the incentive for people to save, borrow, and invest at our bank? How do we move or change from where we are to where and what we want to be?

Many retail bank executives confuse selling with marketing; they point to the vice president of marketing and multimillion dollar ad budgets to prove they are serious about sales. But marketing is a preselling and postselling activity—it attracts customers (more new than old), and should serve to retain customers but good old one-on-one: Personal selling is still the way to close any deal.

One-shot product promotions and seasonal sales campaigns are not the the true measure of a sales culture. Keep in mind that banks are usually not faced with liquidating excess inventories of CDs or loan products.

Selling Strengths and Weaknesses

Selling is an exercise not unlike physical exercise. It needs to be an integral part of the daily life of the organization. Selling, like situps, can rank fairly low on an individual's priority list, however. Some view selling as the practice of persuading people to do something they don't want to do, or that it is cheap, unprofessional, and undignified. Some see a fragmented, undirected sales organization in their bank and figure it can't be that important (or else management would fix it). Others hope that the selling "fad" will die out and

CUSTOMER RETENTION = PROFITABILITY

"Companies can double their profits by keeping just five percent more of their customers."

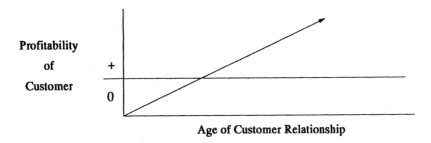

"Harvard Business Review," September-October 1990.

Figure 8–1. Relation between customer retention and profitability. *Source:* Innovative Systems, Inc.

things can revert to the "good old days." They may also think that nickel candy bars will soon be back on the shelves.

Perhaps the weakest link in the retail banking chain is cross-selling. Industry surveys reveal that a customer who holds only one product with a bank stays an average of eight months. Those who have multiple relationships with their bank tend to stay for life or at least until they move. Cross-selling to enrich meaningful customer relationships is much easier to talk about than to achieve. See Figure 8–1.

Vision Plus Vigorous Action

Retail bankers need to demonstrate the entrepreneurial vision and action that has transformed other industries and propelled startup companies to leadership positions. Some bankers have turned their organizational structure around and have instituted effective cross-selling programs that are siphoning customers away from the competition. These are bankers who are not whining about nonbank invasions of their turf, but are competing on their terms and winning.

So just how do you get customers to share more of their wealth and banking needs? How do you turn your bank into an aggressive sales-driven organization? Edward E. Crutchfield, Chairman and CEO of First Union Corporation, believes "the banks that will thrive will be those that reach beyond basic banking functions to build strong broad-based relationships." Crutchfield speaks with resolve about how a sales-driven bank can change its fortunes. In 1985, First Union was a $7 billion state bank; by the end of June, 1991, after acquiring 22 banks along the way, First Union had become a five-state regional superpower with assets topping $39.7 billion.

To develop a successful sales culture requires the total support of everyone from the CEO right down through the ranks. A hierarchical vision forms the foundation of such an institution, where each person understands what the role of selling on their level, the goals for that level, and their individual sales function within that level.

In a sales-driven retail bank, tellers know what, to whom, and why to sell, and are measured and rewarded accordingly. CSRs are similarly trained, with opportunities for greater rewards, since sales efforts are concentrated on the platform. The operations staff, even though they may not contact customers directly, need product knowledge training and a chance at rewards for generating business. Likewise, other personnel, including commercial lenders, branch managers, trust officers, and collectors have their own roles. From top to bottom, each knows his or her opportunity and responsibility and how their piece of the puzzle fits into the financial health and growth of the bank.

Those doing the selling have to understand their customers better in order to succeed. Wholesale bankers have specialized in that function for many years. They dissect the customer's needs, practice making calls, and then spend half an hour or more making calls on corporate treasurers. Retail bankers can't spend that kind of time on each of their customers, but they can make outgoing calls. They need technology to support those calls so they know who they're talking to and what that person's needs are or may be in the near future. They also need to be able to enter the data without getting slowed down by paper and then move on to the next call.

Sales Must Be Driven By Sellers

The low morale among platform personnel (and tellers for that matter) has been a nagging problem facing bankers for generations. Staff turnover of 20 percent and more and unacceptable low levels of productivity provide abundant evidence that a change is badly needed.

The traditional transaction-based heritage of banking favored CSRs who could perform routine service tasks quickly and accurately—and get the customer out of the branch as soon as possible. The bank as sales organization requires much more from those who sell and service. To effectively administer cross-selling, the employees' self-image must change from that of customer order-taker to sales professional. At a recent bank convention, a speaker at a session on platform automation repeatedly referred to CSRs as "clerks." If you keep calling a person a clerk, and treating him or her like a clerk, that individual will act like a clerk.

Let's take a look at four measures that can improve the status of bank employees and motivate superior sales performance:

- The technological support systems
- Automated sales tracking
- Incentive-based compensation
- Professional training/retraining programs

SALES REPORTING SYSTEMS

The degree to which a bank succeeds in transforming itself into a proactive sales-driven operation is the task and the tale of sales and management reporting systems.

Many retail bankers are targeting the so-called "high value" quality customer, the upscale or almost-affluent household. To fuel this growth of the bank and the quest for upscale customers, sales and management reporting systems both direct, and give a richer understanding of, the sales process as practiced by CSRs, telemarketers, and outside calling officers. Branch automation systems can capture this data, sort, sift, and compile the results of the thousands of daily sales encounters at the bank and report those results in meaningful ways for analysis, decision making, and goal setting.

Automation experts say that while automation has been highly successful in cutting production costs for all types of businesses, huge gains can still be made in applying similar processes to marketing and sales functions. Rowland T. Moriarty and Gordon S. Swartz, both of the Harvard Business School, note that sales increases arising from advanced marketing and sales information technology of the late 1980s have ranged from 10 percent to more than 30 percent. Investment returns from these systems have often exceeded 100 percent.

Moriarty and Swartz cite the example of Xerox, which installed an internally developed marketing and sales productivity (MSP) system for its southern region in 1985. Within two years, the system increased sales force productivity by as much as 20 percent and trimmed $3 million off the company's budget. MSPs automate highly repetitive support tasks, such as answering requests for literature and writing letters, and reduce time spent on nonselling tasks like scheduling sales calls, compiling sales reports, and generating proposals. The net result is that salespeople, which bankers have become, can spend more time selling.

Sales Behind the Scenes

American Savings Bank uses a branch automation system from Unisys Corporation. Where did they start implementation? Not on the platform in the branches, but in the telemarketing Bankphone Center in their White Plains, New York headquarters. The telemarketing operators have more of the information they need at their fingertips, and information they can access faster than the bank's platform personnel. The sales representative on the phone can perform instant "what-if" analyses for the call-in customer, quote savings and CD rates without hesitation, and open new accounts. These phonebound sellers gather the same types of information as their platform counterparts: they identify the source of the sales lead, the impact of advertising and direct mail literature, as well as those valuable customer demographics, family data, and banking habits and needs.

Other banks have successfully launched loans by phone programs. And when the customer comes into the bank to sign the loan documents, the CSR does not hesitate to cross sell other products based on the customer information gathered by the telemarketer. These bankers practice the sales sermon they preach—every customer contact is an opportunity to sell.

Start at the Beginning

Every bank needs to assess the current level of sales effectiveness to establish a baseline to measure future sales success. Information is available to determine cross-sell ratios, product profitability, and sales by branch. The goals of the sales program also need to be clearly articulated by bank management and understood by all concerned—and that means CSRs, especially if the program is incentive-based.

In a sales-driven bank, goals for revenue and product growth are constantly compared to actual results. Sales and management reporting systems evolve over time. The information seen as most valuable two years ago is no longer used to measure one bank's primary objectives for next year. Bankers become more and more sophisticated as time go by and sales go up.

Nurturing a Fertile Sales Environment

Industry surveys indicate that by simply tracking sales activity and customer contact information a bank can increase its sales by 20 percent or more. A vice president of marketing says the most eye-opening revelation of sales tracking and reporting systems is that "extraordinary and dismal results become equally known . . . to the penny or hundredth of a percent." The other message is the old adage that "people do what you inspect not what you expect." The act of measuring itself becomes a motivation to perform.

Private bankers, and ultimately their customers, can benefit from sales productivity tools that organize the day-to-day activities of sales officers and help to manage long-term relationships with valued private banking customers. Sales productivity tools can tap into branch automation applications, customer information files, and the bank's MCIF. Lists can be printed based on client characteristics. Management reports can be used to administer performance reviews, identify areas for training or retraining, and to plan and project future sales. Sales tracking programs also capture and maintain a complete customer contact history, which can be summoned at any time for on-screen review or for a printed recap.

Trackstar, a PC-based sales tracking system from Manning Professional Services, tracks sales contacts by first contact date, lead source, address, and tickler date; it can also track and report such data as product(s) sold and mailing codes to better segment and target the ongoing sales effort. The tickler file is an often overlooked, but critically important, ingredient of sales tracking. It keeps potential customers from being lost in the limbo of forgotten opportunities.

The SalesExpert program from Innovative Microsystems has an excellent tickler feature built into its comprehensive appointment calendar. SalesExpert organizes the day-to-day activities of the bank salesperson and is designed to manage the long-term relationship with the bank's most valued private banking customers and/or commercial banking clients. This sales and management tool can tap into branch automation applications, customer information files, and the bank's marketing system. The software enables a salesperson to create lists based on client characteristics, and sort information according to geographic, demographic, and financial criteria. Management reporting functions assess specific campaigns, administer performance reviews, identify areas for training or retraining, and plan and project future sales potential.

Sales tracking programs also capture and maintain a complete customer contact history, which can be summoned at any time for on-screen review or for a printed recap. These programs can even run on laptop PCs so the officer calling on a client outside the bank can have the bank's information resources on hand off-site.

Harvesting the Information

Some bankers monitor and manage the sales scores of individuals, branches, and bankwide, using the reporting functions of their branch automation systems, while other bankers use dedicated sales and management programs linked to branch automation data.

In 1983, San Diego Trust and Savings Bank, a 100-year-old institution with 50 branches, created their own sales and management system called $uccess and sold it to 15 other sales-minded banks. When Unisys installed an FSA/Finesse branch automation system at the bank in 1987, they were so impressed with $uccess that they agreed to jointly market the software to other Unisys customers.

$uccess has been instrumental in enabling San Diego Trust to post some mighty impressive results. After $uccess, average net annual income jumped from $4.6 million to $7.5 million; staff turnover dropped from 10.4 percent to slightly over 4 percent, and the bank's cross-sell ratio moved from a dismal 1.1 to an impressive 2.69.

More than 60 banks have implemented the Motivator, from Resource One for establishing goals, tracking sales, and calculating earned incentives. First Union relies on the Motivator to manage and fine-tune sales strategy and administer the incentive program for the bank's 4,800 participating employees. The bank depends on a battery of reports to monitor teller referrals, assess individual CSR sales activity, and analyze interbranch performance. "The automated system ties the entire program together," said Chief Crutchfield of First Union, "and provides the feedback that is absolutely necessary to run the sales organization."

The Motivator sales and management system provides bankers with a wealth of invaluable information to analyze, evaluate, and redirect the bank's sales efforts. Among the Motivator's management reports are cross-sell ratios by individual, branch (and up to nine organizational levels from district to bankwide), detailed sales analyses showing lead product sold and product(s) cross-sold with new business dollars and incremental amounts; variance from bank goals, and a number of incentive-earned compensation reports. Reports show sales activity for the period and the year-to-date summaries. Ranking by individual, branch, and region are also standard. The system runs through the bank's branch automation software to gather the data for analysis and reporting.

Information is power. The branch automation system routinely gathers information that can turn the bank into an aggressive sales-driven, entrepreneurial institution that serves as a partner to its customers and a leader in its market. The strategic use of sales information builds and develops the skills and talents of the people of the bank, giving them the power to plan, manage and vastly increase sales, revenues, and profits.

REWARD PERFORMANCE

Carrots, Coddling, and Contests

Many banks have experimented with various motivational techniques and incentive programs from offering perks, such as dinners or theater tickets, to top sales performers to running sales contests with prizes or awards for the winners. The elements of a cash incentive or salary plus commission compensation program need to be carefully and completely orchestrated or the program can backfire in a cloud of smoky rebellion, higher staff turnover, and customer confusion and resentment. The entire program needs the commitment of senior management and articulation of the bank's short- and long-range goals and objectives. Other items on the checklist are

- An understanding of the bank's current levels of sales-effectiveness ratios (total products sold divided by customer contacts), product profitability, sales impact, and the strategic areas calling for immediate action.
- Cast the incentive program in "clay," not stone. It must be flexible enough to accommodate change and support a variety of incented schemes.
- Make certain it is easy to understand by the participants.
- Automated tracking and reporting are necessary to ensure proper credit is given for product sales.

To encourage cross-selling specifically, a bank may want to consider not paying a commission or incentive until a second product is sold to the customer, or providing an additional bonus for three or more products sold during a single contact.

Battle of the Heavyweight Banks

Two sales-driven banks, battling for market share and customer loyalty in the great northwest, are **Washington Mutual Savings Bank** and **Pacific First Bank** both headquartered in Seattle. Washington Mutual offers customers all the traditional banking products plus full-service brokerage services, a range of insurance policies, and a travel agency. The bank's executive vice president of retail financial services explained, "the job is not operational, the job is to produce sales and profits." CSRs are called "account representatives."

Everyone participates in the incentive program—a total of 780 employees. Incentives are based on branch profitability and individual performance; bonuses are paid monthly. There are no caps, and star performers can really earn top dollar. The bank adjusted salaries to a sliding scale in 1988 to reflect this approach. While tellers earn 90 percent in base salary, branch managers are assured of just 60 percent, earning the rest in incentives. The Washington Mutual spokesperson added, "don't confuse compensation with management; compensation is the motivator but managers still manage."

Pacific First Bank's financial centers are designed to meet any customer's total financial needs, including saving, borrowing, and investing, through traditional bank products, as well as brokerage and insurance services.

While grappling with the incentive issue in the late 1980s, Pacific First's management couldn't see the value of cutting salaries. The sales manager of the retail banking group said that "cutting salaries seemed like manipulating employees; there is no faster way to kill a program than by reducing salary. Incentives come out of profits. There is no need for the bank to touch salary."

Washington Mutual's incentive-based plan was implemented gradually. It is closely monitored and managed, and adjusted to meet the goals and needs of the bank. "Washington Mutual places more emphasis on market share than cross-selling," said the bank's spokesperson. "We look at market penetration and increasing the number of relationships per household and plan our strategies accordingly."

Pacific First believed the bank's success was evident in the average number of relationships with customers. An initial jump in relationships indicated great success with the incentive program, but management and staff soon found itself concentrating too much on high scores.

"We were using sales effectiveness ratios (SERs) to reward sales performance," noted Pacific First's manager of sales planning, "but it defeated the idea of a relationship-based selling environment." By using their customer information file to determine relationships with individuals and households, Pacific First redirected their focus on the customer's long-term needs. Those relationships are based on product bundling, such as a checking account, savings account, overdraft protection, and ATM card.

"We're getting a lot better about dealing with the customers," added Pacific First's manager of sales planning. "We knew if we did that, our SERs would increase on their own, which they have. A few years ago we were operating at an SER of 1.8; after two years we nearly doubled it to 3.26." Pacific First's managers also do a lot of informal recognition of performance, including sending notes, making phone calls, and using other types of recognition and praise."

Both banks use telemarketing to build sales and extend customer relationships, and both devote considerable attention to ongoing sales training and retraining programs.

The Fruits of Sales Labors

Well-tuned sales programs at many banks feature an incentive or bonus compensation component for individuals and "branch teams." Some banks have an incentive program that rewards the cross-selling job of the CSRs for all consumer and mortgage products. In one approach, using an asset/liability model, points are assigned to products based on their profitability. Monthly commissions are based on point scores after a CSR exceeds the benchmark cross-sell ratio.

According to James Towns, vice president at Resource One, the "hallmark of the Motivator software is flexibility. It accommodates a variety of sales incentive options from cash commissions to point and award programs." Computation of cross-sell bonuses are a standard function of the system. It also tracks leads and referrals, records product sales, and does comparisons and trend analysis at the local, regional, and corporate levels.

Cross-sell ratios are only one benchmark of a bank's success in sales. Mickey Newbury, president of Resource One, described a trend among sales-oriented banks: "While many bankers stress cross-sell ratios in the beginning, they soon start looking at other data to measure results, such as product profitability, types of customers served, and the variety of products that form customer relationships." Newbury summarized this management information as "sales performance value."

Incorporating sales reporting, incentives, and management reporting into the branch automation system enables branch managers to review sales on a weekly basis. They can respond quickly to potential problems and praise exemplary sales achievements days after they happen. Senior managers appreciate the sales summaries by region and by product within regions. Tracking market receptivity to new product introductions by the new-account opening patterns at different branches provides valuable added information for advertising and promotion plans.

The ability to see management reports graphically is high on the wish list of many bankers. Charts and graphs enable managers to more easily spot meaningful trends than they can by sifting through pages of spreadsheet statistics. Highlight meaningful information in color on the PC screen, and graph the sales trends according to bank-defined criteria.

ALL ABOARD THE TRAINING EXPRESS

Sales training or retraining is not a one-shot deal. It should be an ongoing program that fosters the sales culture. Training means developing the habits, attitudes, and behaviors of seasoned sales pros in addition to imparting new product knowledge. Branch managers and supervisors also require new skills to coach sales performance and motivate employees to excel.

Several fallacies exist about motivation, and it would be good not to let yourself fall within their grasp. Money, for example, is commonly thought of as the prime carrot with which to motivate employees. Experts note, however, that this myth is true up to a point, but if your staff are well compensated but lack other nonmonetary aspects in their jobs, they may still be unhappy. Punishment is an easy fallback option, but behavioral scientists have shown that negative reinforcement doesn't change behavior as readily as positive reinforcement. Also, you can't see motivation, but you can see its results, which is productivity. A manager's job is to produce the latter, while providing the environment for the former.

In a recent study of retail banking delivery systems conducted by the Bank Administration Institute, training and retraining ranked high on bankers' "must-do" lists. Among the key actions to be implemented were "developing managers, increasing the emphasis on new employee training, and revamping of employee skills for changing jobs and organizational needs."

Cross-selling is a people skill that can be learned, developed, and refined, given experience and training. Remember, we are assuming there is a solid branch automation system in place that supports the CSRs' selling efforts and streamlines administrative operations. We are also assuming that CSRs have a firm understanding of the features and benefits of the bank's products and fee-based services.

A training program to groom the CSR, or telemarketing representative, needs to focus on such areas as communication and probing skills to identify and elicit customer needs, eliminating the fear of selling, defining sales skills that the individual already possesses and teaching new sales techniques, and developing time management skills.

Automated Training Aids

Grabbing the headlines in the field of training and development these days is computer-based training (CBT), that is, the use of computers to educate employees in a wide range of subjects.

In 1990, for example, Wells Fargo Bank installed a CBT program for their 24-hour telephone customer services area. Written in-house to run on the bank's mainframe, the CBT offers training modules from 30 minutes to an hour long. These programs teach bank agents how to use computer application programs, such as retrieving customer information and handling customer inquiries. While the bank continues to train new hirees in the classroom, the CBT has been most useful in teaching new skills or improving current ones with experienced agents. The computer program works through problems using examples and exercises based on real situations.

Other banks have found a place for CBT as well. The Bank of America distributes training for employees who handle their CIFs on the bank's Customer Online Information Network (COIN). The PC-based courseware can be pulled up from the mainframe without having to use a floppy disk, and COIN's IBM PS/2 machines allow users to take advantage of the programs' color and graphic features.

Smaller banks like the CBT approach as well. The $5 billion Chase Lincoln First Bank of Rochester, New York, uses CBT for over half the 80 hours a year of training given to their technical staff. As part of the Chase Manhattan network of banks, Chase Lincoln has programmers, computer operators, and business analysts in Rochester, New York; Phoenix, Arizona; Baltimore, Maryland; and Columbus, Ohio. CBT becomes especially valuable when staff students are widely dispersed geographically, since they save travel money and allow employees flexibility on where and when they study.

Chase Lincoln has also moved into "authoring" its own programs, whereby they can either modify off-the-shelf software to their own specifications or write their own. The bank has plans for as many as 100 such courses during the 1990s.

Keeping students interested is one of the key prerequisites of any successful training program, including CBTs. The hot ticket in the market these days are interactive videodisks (IVD). Simply put, the IVD combines computer graphics and videofilm into a multimedia package that can be both entertaining and educational. The students use a touch screen to proceed through the lessons.

"The difference from just a videotape," says Judy Steele, senior program director for Learning International, one of the world's largest training companies, "is that it branches into different paths depending on what you touch on the screen"

In 1989, Learning International launched an IVD product called Sales Challenge, a five-part course designed to reinforce face-to-face selling skills. Among their target audience were bankers.

"Many people in banking haven't been market-oriented," says Steele. "They may not have been hired for those skills or trained extensively in them; yet, as banking has become more competitive, they've been pushed into that role. They receive periodic classroom training, and the Sales Challenge is designed to fill in the gaps between those sessions." The Sales Challenge requires a PC with a touch-screen monitor, as well as a videodisk player (see photo below).

Among the first banks to use the Sales Challenge product was Sovran Financial Corporation now part of Nations Bank. The head of the training department selected a group of line managers to take part in the pilot program in late 1989. Managers were assessed in their ability to handle sales calls as a starting point. The IVD was then made available to them for ten weeks. At the conclusion, they performed video exercises to test their selling skills. The results showed a definite increase in confidence.

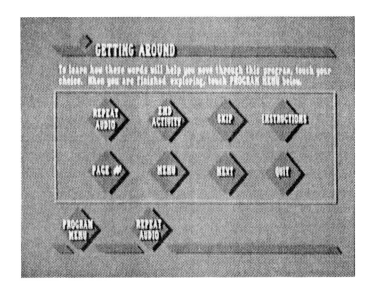

Training by satellite television also appears to be imminent at several banks. Such programs would piggyback on data transmission networks, and would lend themselves to special training situations—for example, when you have one expert who has a consistent message to deliver and a critical time period in which to get the information out. Another scenario would be training all your branch employees on a new product. You can put an expert on the satellite and have branch people call in their questions by telephone.

The increase in technology in the banking world, as in the rest of the world, has put an additional emphasis on training and retaining those who deal with that technology. Bankers Trust, the New York-based investment bank, spent 3.5 years studying the issue of hiring and holding on to qualified "techies." They concluded, in part, that the long-term health of their institution, and banks in general, depends on keeping the automation systems, and those who manage them, happy.

"We think there are tremendous efficiencies to be gained through technology," noted a vice president of human resources, "but they will come from people." Part of the Bankers Trust study included interviews with employees leaving the bank, many of whom stated that they were exiting not because of money or the environment but because they felt there were more career opportunities elsewhere. By building training curriculums that include possibilities of advancement at your bank, you can hope to retain those people.

Are You Sold on Selling?

A bank, like any other business organization, is a creature of its environment and a creature of habit. On the outside, the environment has become increasingly competitive and deregulated. Hungry nonbanks are encroaching on your turf with new financial services that are enticing your customers. At the same time, customers are getting more sophisticated, more demanding, and more critical. They expect value-added service for their dollars.

Because the times are a-changing, the internal environment of the bank must change. It must evolve to serve and sell better than it has in the past. It must spawn a sales culture to pursue growth and future success, not to mention survival. Making sales the mission of everyone can turn a ho-hum bank into a star performer.

A sales organization does not grow overnight. It needs a hothouse of nurturing, commitment, and integrated planning to thrive and prosper. The image and role of CSRs need to change. They deserve respect, they are the ones who will make or break the sales organization.

But remember, you are in this business for the long haul. Remember the sales-as-exercise analogy. The more you do it, the better you feel, and the better you look to yourself, your employees, your stockholders, and your customers.

9

Branch Bank Merchandising

Those solid brick and mortar branches with lobbies of towering marble columns and thick steel vault doors have actually served a useful purpose. After the massive bank failures of the 1890s and 1930s, the American public needed reassurance that they were putting their money in a safe place. The appearance of solidity and trustworthiness was as important as any other phase of banking. The image of the staid banker, one who could even act with some imperiousness toward customers, fit snugly into that mold.

Deregulation, courtesy of the federal government, changed all that. The Depository Institutions Deregulation and Monetary Control Act of 1980 and the Garn-St Germain Depository Institutions Act of 1982 opened a floodgate of new products and services. Nonfinancial institutions like J. C. Penney and Sears, Roebuck and Co. began to compete for depositors' dollars. Banking's quasi-monopoly began to rapidly disintegrate. No longer could financial institutions rely on a healthy profit margin simply by accepting funds and making loans. No longer could bankers simply focus on providing reliable transactions and enough staff to handle customer flows. No longer was the banker's credo: Open at 10 A.M., close at 3 P.M., and tee off at 4 P.M.

Branch banks remain the primary channel for delivering retail banking. to branches and customers. They are the channel that provides the convenience and service that customers need and want in order to keep their finances healthy and in order.

However, just by opening the doors in the morning, bankers are not assured that crowds will rush in. In fact, going to the bank for many Americans ranks as a necessary chore somewhere near a visit to the dentist and paying taxes. It's not hard to find someone who can tell you a retail banking horror story at the slightest provocation. Surly tellers, nonfunctioning equipment, lost signature cards—these are personal recollections of trips to the local bank branch that went sour. On the other side of the desk, bank personnel often view customers as potential headaches with which they have to deal. The increase in part-time tellers, who work without benefits and who expect—and are expected—to remain only a short time with the bank obviates most feelings of loyalty to the financial institution. Such an atmosphere does not engender good customer service.

Learning how to pull customers in or at least off the sidewalk is an art in which few bankers were trained before the mid-1980s. By looking to retail merchandisers, some of whom have become direct competitors, bankers have begun to apply many lessons to their own environment.

BANK RETAILING

Focus on the Customer

Bank merchandising can be defined as the display of products or information about those products. Effective merchandising of retail banking products creates customer interest or even the urge to buy.

Everyday examples of merchandising abound, such as walking through a sporting goods store and seeing a picture of a sports star rising above the crowd with a certain brand of sneakers on his or her feet. Or seeing a display for a new spy thriller in the bookstore that almost forces you to pick up a copy of the book and start reading. Even though the customer may have been shopping for next year's calendar and a novel for his or her mother, the merchandiser supplies the urge to add the page turner to the customer's basket.

Retail merchandising, in many cases, satisfies an *immediate* want. The customer can buy those sneakers and be on the basketball court within minutes. Amnother customer can spend the afternoon reading that book. The retailer, through the stimulation of sounds, sights, smells, and service, creates the desire for a tangible product.

As in any industry, retailing has had to change with the times. Department stores, for example, used to try to be all things to all people, carrying a broad range of products. Success came easily to these mass merchandising operations. So easy, in fact, that they didn't keep track of changes in their customers. Most notably, middle-age and older populations grew markedly as the Baby Boom bulge worked its way through successive decades. *Barnard's Retail Marketing Report* publisher Kurt Barnard, quoted in *Fortune* magazine, says that "Retailers had done so well for the past 20 years almost without paying attention to market changes. Now they have to."

As competition increased, so did the retailers' sophistication. Retailers now sell not just a product, but "style" and "fashion" as well. They also found the need to focus and specialize in order to differentiate themselves from the competition. The environment of the store has become almost as important as the items on sale. "The buzzword of the eighties (was) focus," retail merchandiser John Curran told the *San Francisco Business Times*. "You have to get your message across because people want to make their decisions quickly and get on." Curran's clients include such successful retailers as Williams-Sonoma, Eddie Bauer, Fanny Farmer, and Brooks Brothers.

Make the Offer Tangible

While the goal of enticing customers to buy remains the same for retail banking, the "product" being sold is less tangible, sometimes not well understood, and often hard to even see. Not only that, most financial goods and services don't offer *immediate* gratification. They are future-oriented, and rely on the institutions's faith and goodwill to deliver down the road. Speaking at an NCR-sponsored conference on "Bankers As Retailers," Dan Dorsey of the design firm Fitch Richardson Smith put it this way: "Basically, as bankers, what we are asking customers to do is to give us their money and sometime in the future they will see a benefit out of it . . ., maybe."

Dorsey explained that, although banking and retailing aren't all that far apart, he has noted one graphic difference. Sitting at home on a Saturday morning, he may suddenly have the urge to gather his wife and kids and go shopping for a new car. Never, however, has he blurted out the words, "Honey, get the kids. We're going banking."

From a logical point of view, banking occupies as important a place in our lives as new stereos and bedsheets, but, as Dorsey points out, we haven't been accustomed to treating it that way. The fact is that banking and our money form much of the framework of our lives. Why couldn't it be as exciting as buying a new outfit or a gift for the kids? "The irony," added Dorsey, "is that retailers add the intangible to the offer, while bankers are trying to make their offer tangible."

Just as marketing is not the same as selling, merchandising does not equate to advertising. Rather, merchandising is the presentation of products and information in three-dimensional space in a way that allows customers to interact with that information and the bank's employees. Put another way, your merchandising efforts should result in waypoints within your branch environment by which customers can navigate their way to what they need and want by way of financial services.

All Aboard at Dollar Dry Dock

One bank that received attention for their considerable efforts in this arena was New York's **Dollar Dry Dock Bank.** Drawing heavily from the principles of retailing, the bank set about transforming their 23 traditional branches into state-of-the-art financial centers in 1986. According to the bank's former director of marketing Linda Lockhart, previously a merchandise manager and buyer for Bloomingdale's, the bank applied the four principles of merchandising: *Product, Place, Promotion,* and *People.*

Any retailer will tell you that having the right product assortment is crucial to success, especially those products that cater to the key market segments in your customer population. By taking advantage of New York State's savings bank laws, Dollar Dry Dock was able to offer a broad range of financial services and products. They included securities, real estate brokerage, mutual funds, insurance, mortgages, consumer loans, travel, and foreign currency exchange.

Upgrading Dollar Dry Dock's dark and gloomy branch offices required considerable research and rethinking. Interviews with customers revealed that they wanted a friendly, nonintimidating and comfortable space that exuded a feeling of good service and efficiency. Cold marble just isn't going to cut it in the new age of banking.

Step one in improving branch appearance was to remove clutter from the doors, windows, floors, and ceilings. Waist-high sales counters like you would find at a department store replaced sit down desks as the initial point of customer contact. Employees interact proactively with customers at these locations, moving to sales stations if and when the customer decides that's what he or she wants to do.

Laying out the flow of traffic in the branch provided opportunities to promote the bank's range of products. By placing the teller stations in the rear of the lobby, the bank drew customers through the entire rainbow of services offered at the branch.

"Although the customer may not be in the market for a mutual fund that day," said Lockhart, "we hope that when they recognize that need in their financial life, they will remember that we had a mutual fund department. . . . We are hoping that if they were happy with their service for the past 10 or 20 years, that they would trust us with their other financial services."

(Continued)

Promotion extended outside the branch, via large picture windows and signage that shouted, lured or otherwise created interest. Bright colors attracted the eye, especially on banners and brochures. To add more theatricality to their presentation, Dollar Dry Dock also installed inside the branch an electronic "data wall" measuring approximately nine feet by six feet. In addition to presenting information about the bank's services, the data wall presented value-added data, including the prime rate, gold and silver prices, foreign currency exchange rates, and a Dow Jones News ticker tape. Each financial center had at least two video monitors run centrally off laser disk technology. Like the data wall, these screens presented programs on bank products as well as general information from *Wall Street Week*.

Finally, Dollar Dry Dock focused on the quality of personal interactions between the bank and its customers. The bank wanted to recognize their customers as guests and seize the opportunity to get to know them better, something that doesn't happen every day in New York City. The employee playing this role was to serve as a greeter, not unlike a maitre d' at a restaurant, and to make the customer welcome. In addition, the greeter pointed them in the right direction for completing whatever transaction brought them into the branch.

The position of "information assistant" was created in 1988 near the completion of the branch overhauls. According to Lockhart, "I don't know how we ever managed without this individual." In addition to greeting customers, the information assistant kept track of the merchandising systems within the branch, including posters, laser disks, and brochures.

"If you looked inside a Dollar Dry Dock financial center in the morning," she said, "it looked like a department store. They were dusting the shelves and getting ready to open up the doors for the customers."

Dollar Dry Dock's transformation had immediate impact. Deposit growth increased by a whopping 134 percent in 1989, while fees from nontraditional products rose by an impressive 68 percent. The bank added over 18,000 new customers in the year following the conversions, an increase of more than 40 percent over the previous year. Unfortunately, this retail success was not matched by the lending side of the institution, which fell prey to the nonperforming loanitis that plagued banks in the Northeast in the early 1990s. Dollar Dry Dock was acquired by New York's Emigrant Savings Bank in 1992.

BRANCHES AS COMMUNICATION AND MEDIA CENTERS

In addition to continuing its role as a place to conduct routine transactions, the bank branch must also become known for creating value in the relationship banking process. The branch needs to offer information that the customer will either use immediately or in the future.

The hallmark of today's consumer is education. We are literally swamped with information about our world. We have learned to become more inquisitive about the goods and services that are being offered to us. We have also become more savvy to "vendor-driven" ploys to buy not what we need, but what the seller wants us to buy. Banks will succeed if they can attract customers with 'needs-driven' services.

Merchandising provides banks with the tools with which they can communicate information to customers. In the process, successful merchandising also creates an identity which distinguishes your bank from the competition. A year-long merchandising calendar, not unlike an advertising calendar, should be designed to reinforce this distinct identity.

Think of your branch as a form of media, like television, radio, or newspaper. Consumer traffic becomes the viewing audience. You have many opportunities to create "impressions," to use a term often associated with media buyers. According to the *Ryan Report on Retail Banking* prepared by John Ryan & Company, a retail marketing agency that has installed merchandising services in 6,000 bank branches around the world, the cost per thousand impressions for in-branch merchandising in the late 1980s was as low as 10 cents. At the time, that was 75 percent less than television advertising.

Branch as media has other advantages over mass media.

Instead of trying to reach a broad audience, your inhouse merchandising campaigns target a very qualified customer base. You, not the editorial staff of a newspaper or television station programmers, control the placement, frequency, and content of your promotions. You can pinpoint campaigns to different customer demographics. Consider also that in-branch merchandising can't be zapped by the remote control button.

The study of behavior in retail environments has become in many ways a science, not that far removed, in fact, from cultural anthropology or sociology. Firms like Envirosell, Inc., a behavioral research company, films shoppers to determine traffic patterns and responses to point of purchase advertising and displays. The firm's clientele includes everything from manufacturers, to retail chains, trade associations, real estate developers, and retail banks.

Banks that have taken advantage of Envirosell's expertise include such notables as Citibank, NationsBank, Security Pacific Bank, Wells Fargo Bank and Home Savings Bank of America. When auditing such an institution, the firm uses videocameras to observe and quantify such elements as

- The number and quality of exposure presented to customers by each element of merchandising, from teller line kiosks and posters to brochure presentation positions
- The degree of customer penetration into all public areas of the branch
- The percentage of customers who interact with collateral material
- A comparison of exposure rates and quality of exposure to in-branch merchandising compared to national sample
- Average times spent by customers in the branch and at the teller and platform stations
- The percentage of customers in the bank who use a teller
- How long, at different hours of the day, customers have to wait to see a platform officer

Envirosell's research shows that the more you understand and cater to your customers, the greater will be your profits. Pushing the decision-making process as close to the shop floor creates the most positive results. Generating sales is an ongoing process of tuning the relationship between planning, operations, and marketing.

Arranging Your Environment

Effective merchandising represents a marriage of science and art, not to mention a healthy serving of common sense. In setting up your branch banking space to get your message across, the most valuable tools you possess are your own perceptions. Imagine yourself as a customer at your bank, or get the input from those who are, to find out what works about your merchandising presentation. Here are some general principles to keep in mind (See Figure 9-1).

Conceptual Teller's Desk

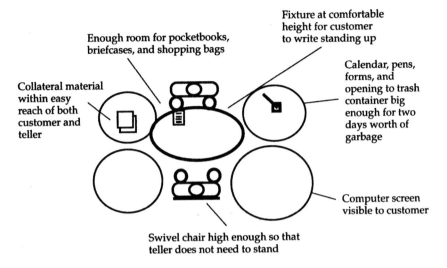

Conceptual Check Ledge

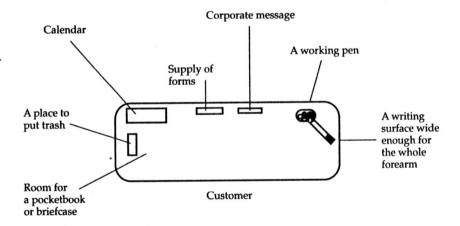

Figure 9–1. Arranging your environment.

- *Allow customers some time to adjust.* Upon entering the branch from the street, it takes a few moments for the customer to slow down, for their eyes to adjust to indoor lighting and for them to orient themselves. By placing displays or promotional signage further into the bank/store, you can dramatically increase interaction on the part of customers.
- *Pay attention to placement.* Bankers tend to be a very transaction-oriented activity. Yet customers want to get their check deposited or make a savings withdrawal and they usually make a beeline to the place where they can get it done. Once a customer completes the task that brought him or her into the bank/store, however, he or she slows down and becomes more receptive to considering other purchases. Orienting your merchandising displays with this in mind can make a difference in how they're received. For brochures, use displays that make it easy to pick up collateral material. Since 70 percent of all customers are right-handed, it makes sense to put a brochure display on the right side of the departure path.
- *Make your displays easy to service so they'll last.* Don't just consider how your merchandising efforts will appear on day one of your promotional campaign. Brochure displays need to be serviced if they are to maintain their attractiveness. If it's difficult to restock or clean up a display, chances are it won't get done.
- *Work the angles.* Give customers a chance to see your signage from a distance, so as they approach the teller area, for example, the impression will have a chance to sink in. Use two-sided or triangular displays, which will permit viewing from an angle, not just head on. Also, overhead signage, which has proven to be effective in retail banking, should be placed so that those standing in line can see it without having to perform an exotic yoga posture. Don't put a message that takes 12 seconds to read and comprehend in an area where customers may only spend three seconds walking by.
- *Help customers become more educated.* If you're going to impinge on your customer's time, it's best to do it with something of value. Tell them exactly how much your auto loan will save them compared to another vendor's. Offering more savvy about financial products so that they will feel that they're coming from a position of strength when they request information about your services.

Moving Pictures and In-Branch Video

Like it or not, the increasing presence of video and multimedia will continue to find its way into our lives more frequently. Retail merchants are already preparing for interactive video shopping facilities. Sitting at a central station or in a private booth, customers will touch a screen to indicate their interest in a certain product. A 3-D graphics program will detail the available merchandise. The customer can then make their selection and either pay by credit or have the amount subtracted from their bank account. An automated delivery system will deliver the purchase to a central pickup point.

While such applications may eventually find their way into banking, the technology of video is already available to aid in merchandising the bank's products and services. In-branch television can be highly effective and cost efficient in getting your message across, although some thought needs to go into the content and length of video clips, and how they fit into the overall marketing strategy.

Bank merchandisers must not confuse in-branch video ads or promotions with the same thing they see on television at home. In the latter situation, assuming the viewer doesn't go to the kitchen for a beer or hit the mute button, advertisements are the main focus. In a branch environment, with other people, signage and daily concerns, viewers are much more distracted. In-store video is more like an electronic poster, and should be perceived as such. Paco Underhill of Envirosell notes in *Marketing News* that customers spend an average of 15 seconds on a video display. With such a short time to make an impact, it doesn't pay to hold back. Music and interchanges between people are the best hooks to capture viewers' attention.

Serving Consumers

Banks have lost market share in recent years because they haven't been as responsive to customer needs as their nonbank competitors. Experts in banking and consumer behavior foresee the 1990s as a time of consumer discontent and increasing pessimism. Many Americans have become concerned about maintaining their standard of living in the face of reduced earning power.

This outlook has fostered an era of strategic shopping. Consumers are becoming more demanding, more discriminating, more results-oriented, and more risk-averse. They want to control risk. At the same time, they want to make more money. Financial institutions that can help solve this conundrum will be the winners as the millenium approaches.

Author Stanley M. Davis in his book *Future Perfect* says that the answer is "mass-customizing," which means that you must "standardize the commodity and and customize the services that surround it."

In-branch merchandising can help achieve this goal. Branches must serve the needs of their surrounding locations. Banks must make full use of their available space, including merchandising that targets their customers and helps customer service. The branch staff must be properly trained and motivated to perform that service. Branches must also provide not only product information, but how those financial goods and services fit into the customers' needs.

BRANCHES OF THE FUTURE

Where the branch was once a concentration of human effort focused on completing customer transactions, it has become more automated with advancing technology and less personal. John Russell, a senior vice president and director of marketing at Banc One Corporation, observed recently in *Bankers Monthly* that these changes have created a lot of extra floor space.

"More than half of our transaction volume takes place outside the branch, either at drive-in windows, ATMs, or through electronic point-of-sale terminals," Russell said. "We've driven people out, leaving us with a storefront that's used only 40 percent of the time."

A leader in field of creating financial centers based around their branches, Banc One has combined numerous outside vendors for real estate, brokerage, small-business lending, travel, and tax and legal services under one roof. By mid-1990, they had a dozen such centers in operation. The branches resemble a mini-shopping mall, relying heavily on merchandising, including wall and ceiling hangings, neon lights, and even pop music. Results have been encouraging. According to Russell, a 6,000 square foot branch near Columbus, Ohio has 25 percent more foot traffic than a standard branch.

Banc One looked to the success of convenience stores in structuring its layouts for their financial centers. They put the "milk," that is, the teller stations, at the rear, forcing customers to walk through a gauntlet of offerings. Although mortgages and tax accountants don't fall into the same category of impulse buying as a box of crackers, exposure to the added services works its way into the customer's mind, which is exactly where the banker/retailer wants to be.

The presence of different vendors, especially ones who rely on evening and weekend hours of business, adds new dimensions to the banker's life. Banc One's financial centers are open from 7 A.M. to 10 P.M. weekdays and shorter hours on both Saturday and Sunday. Recruiting bankers to work on Sunday can be a difficult chore, but Russell has discovered, once again, that the place to look is your nearest retail shopping mall. Training salespeople to be bankers, he has found, can be easier than the opposite approach.

It's important for bankers to realize that by taking initiative in the arena of branch merchandising, especially the inclusion of outside vendors in the retail banking store layout, they can control their destiny. Assuming the concept of financial centers takes hold, there will be third party operators eager to get in on the action. Instead of being landlords, bankers will find themselves as tenants with all the accompanying tribulations.

Downsizing is another alternative. ATMs, computers, and telephones make it possible to concentrate the work of a branch in to a smaller area, or even relocate it elsewhere. Some banks are using a "hub-and-wheel" format, with a full-service branch anchoring an array of smaller branches offering limited services. Perhaps the big winners will be those banks that can adapt their branch strategies to different market segments and build the appropriate infrastructures equipped with targeted merchandising programs.

The push to migrate customers to self-service devices has continued unabated in some sectors. The Money Access Center (MAC) Network, a progressive, regional network stretching from Pennsylvania to New England, recently initiated its MAC Icon service. Extensively tested by CoreStates Financial Corporation at their Newtown, Pennsylvania, branch of Philadelphia National Bank, the MAC machines can record individual check deposits, provide funds drawn on that same check, and print out receipts listing the individual checks and the banks on which they were drawn (see photo next page).

These super ATMs, developed by a consortium of East Coast banks along with NCR and IBM, will also allow customers to perform a range of sophisticated services, including moving funds to multiple accounts, making payments and purchasing financial products such

as certificates of deposit. One machine will reportedly handle the same workload as two tellers, which would free bank staff to concentrate on cross-selling.

Other hardware producers have been tackling the self-service issue. ISC-Bunker Ramo, a division of Olivetti, has explored touch screens, animation, and video for future use. According to Mike Ehrenberg, director of systems and technology planning for ISC-Bunker Ramo, the recent emphasis has been on switching from controller-based systems, which feed information to dumb terminals, to more open systems utilizing personal computers and other, more interactive, devices. With this new technology, vendors can focus on what bankers need, not on how to deliver it.

Those who are producing furniture and other office equipment are adapting to the changing tides. Steelcase, a leading producer of office furniture, offers a free-standing desk with curvilinear shapes that they have found to be more customer friendly than the old rectangular style. Steelcase has also been developing modular teller counters that can be rearranged and moved, unlike traditional, fixed millwork structures.

Red Pope of Arizona's Valley National Bank warns that there is no generic branch of the future. Not all customers are yet comfortable with the high-tech approach to banking. "We're dealing with different market segments," he said. "Some people still want high touch, not high tech. They want a bank to look and sound like a bank, not a supermarket or a video store."

The one constant, of course, is change. However you focus your branch network, with whatever merchandising format, you must be ready to adapt, change, and improve. Major retailers have certain elements of their stores which are relatively permanent, but many more are quite fluid and capable of change. Managing change must become an integral part of ongoing planning.

Urban Solutions: Get Off the Streets!

In urban areas such as Chicago and New York, where street front real estate can be prohibitively expensive, **Citibank** has adopted the idea of "duplex banking," a program it started in 1990.

Instead of trying to put all of its services on sidewalk level, the bank places its high-volume transaction facilities, mostly ATMs, on the ground floor. A half-dozen or more machines can be installed so as to minimize space requirements. One flight up, where rents go down, the bank spreads other branch functions over additional square footage, including private areas for doing business.

According to Citibank, this "split-level" approach to branch banking costs a half to a third as much as the same size layout would cost if it was all located on the street level.

Plan Your Work and Work Your Plan

The changes to the traditional banking environment described in this chapter make the end of the century a pivotal time. New products, new designs and new approaches will affect the consumer's perception of financial industries. Marble and solemnity are being replaced by user-friendly flow patterns and an air of retail theatricality. Moving into this new territory requires some careful thought and planning.

Primary among a banker's thoughts must be the retention of traditional banking values, even if it means doing it with modern techniques. Banking customers are looking for strength, integrity, and trust. Anything that runs counter to those elements will weaken the financial institution's position. Furthermore, bankers must achieve a balance between the retailing and banking, one with which both they and their customers feel comfortable.

Planning, then, becomes a critical element in the progression. Industry experts urge bankers to clarify their position regarding "high tech" and "high touch." The former relies on automation and machinery to service customers, while the latter focuses on *human interaction*. Each or both can be appropriate for different market segments, and banks that straddle customer groups in both need to identify where and how much of their resources they want to devote to each.

Organizing tasks within the bank should be analyzed. Back office functions, such as proofing, bookkeeping, or loan documentation production, can be centralized to free up floor space in branches or allow branches to be smaller. With less floor space, bankers can think of positioning themselves in high-traffic retail locations like shopping centers and malls.

Tools exist to evaluate areas such as queue and teller management, the results of which can help optimize the balance between efficiency and service. Crowe Chizek & Company offers software programs that, combined with automated data gathering equipment, provide reports and statistics about customer use of bank staff. The Queue and Teller Management System (QTMS) establishes teller staffing requirements based on customer service standards and predicted customer traffic. The Computer Aided Teller Scheduling system (CATS) matches anticipated customer traffic with available tellers to produce daily teller schedules. Use of such tools can improve customer service, reduce staffing requirements, increase the accuracy of customer information and help bank management establish customer service standards (see Table 9–1).

The Big Picture

In a recent *Bank Management* survey about banking in the year 2015, Robert Hedges of the MAC Group noted that "service quality and a focus on markets and customers will be primary areas for bankers to address in the near future." Creating a sales culture at the branch

Table 9–1.   Crowe Chizek Lobby Window Wait Time

```
               *   Teller Staffing Report        Monday Low Traffic
                   ============================
                            Sample
                Average Transaction Time:    1.4 Minutes
                Maximum Allowable Average Wait:  2.0 Minutes
```

					--- AVG WAIT ---					
	ARRIV.	TELLERS	%	ALL	FOR THOSE	PROB. OF WAITING OVER				
HOUR	RATE	REQD.	UTIL	CUST	WHO WAIT	0	1	2	3	5(min)
9:00	38	2	45%	0.4	1.3	28	13	6	3	1
10:00	37	2	44%	0.3	1.3	27	12	6	3	1
11:00	24	1	57%	1.9	3.3	57	42	31	23	13
12:00	34	2	40%	0.3	1.2	23	10	4	2	0
1:00	34	2	40%	0.3	1.2	23	10	4	2	0
2:00	41	2	49%	0.4	1.4	32	15	8	4	1
3:00	49	2	58%	0.7	1.7	43	24	13	7	2
4:00	2	1	5%	0.1	1.5	5	2	1	1	0
TOTAL	259		42%							

Crowe Chizek uses the Queue and Teller Management System (QTMS trademark) software by Alternative Management Services, Inc. of Santa Ynez, California to automatically collect data that are used to create staffing plans that balance efficiency and service.

level has become increasingly important to financial institutions' marketing departments. Industry leaders emphasize the importance of initiating strategic thinking by understanding customers.

Since merchandising is new to most bankers, seeking advice from outside consultants makes sense. These experts can recommend retail packages and which branches need full, partial, or no reconfigurations. They can also target the most likely branches to produce the highest return on investment from a makeover and implementation of a merchandising strategy.

"There are certain economics that make retrofitting economical," notes Tom Pritzker with John Ryan & Co. "If you're Bank of America . . ., you won't rebuild them all as branches of the future. Retrofitting is more feasible and timely. Plus, a bank's need for profit and meeting shareholders' demands make those expenditures harder to justify."

No branch is an island unto itself.

It is part of a bank's regional, statewide, or institutionwide sales and delivery system. Branch merchandising isn't a panacea, and shouldn't be considered one. It should be considered a *tool*, a part of the banker's workbench, which also includes training and sales, platform automation, direct mail marketing, and other proactive sales elements.

10

Breaking Banking Barriers

The time-worn adage that "you can't teach an old dog new tricks" touches on a fundamental truth of human behavior: once we become used to a certain way of doing things, we resist change, even if that transformation will benefit us in the long run. Yet, if anything has characterized the world of financial institutions over the past decade, it is that adapting to change is crucial to fiscal health, not to mention survival.

Here is one of the most simple, yet vivid, examples of how we box ourselves into conventional thinking, and thereby limit ourselves from finding creative solutions to problems. On a piece of paper, draw three rows of three dots, creating a square that looks like that in Figure 10–1. Without removing your pencil from the paper, connect the nine dots by using just four straight lines.

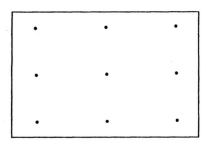

Figure 10–1. Connect the dots problem.

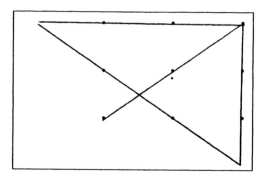

Figure 10–2.   Connect the dots solution.

Most people, when confronted with this puzzle, will try to connect the dots without venturing outside the imaginary box they describe. Note, however, that the instructions do not limit you from extending those lines beyond the imagined rectangle, which, in fact, is the only way to successfully complete the puzzle (see Figure 10–2).

Venturing "outside the nine dots" represents an allegory for what retail bankers can do to forge creative responses to the challenges facing the financial services industry. The PA Consulting Group, an international management and technology consulting firm, recently polled top U.S. and Canadian banks and identified those challenges as:

- New and increasing competition from both foreign-owned and nonbank players
- Regulatory uncertainty
- Cost pressures
- A move towards a service economy
- An ever-shrinking pool of adequately educated workers

In response to these pressures, banks have begun to recognize the need to enhance their service quality, reduce their expenses, and maximize the responsiveness of their delivery systems to consumer needs. Of the executives polled by the PA Consulting Group, almost 9 out of 10 said they needed business and technology solutions that will provide a lasting advantage in the marketplace. Many of them added that these solutions would require "breakout" creativity.

If only the answers were as easy as connecting the nine dots! Some bankers have, however, demonstrated that breakout creativity can lead to breakthrough customer service and enhanced profitability.

SUPERMARKET BRANCHING

Lettuce Be Your Banker

According to a 1989 customer survey by the Food Marketing Institute (FMI), more than 30 percent of America's supermarket shoppers would use full-service banking if it were available. Of those shoppers who had full-service banks in their stores—there were over 1,200 of these banks in December 1991—one out of three said they used the bank "frequently or occasionally." (See Figure 10–3.) Although past FMI surveys showed that in-store banking was one of the services shoppers wanted to see most, full-service banks in supermarkets remain relatively new. The prospects continue to be exceedingly bright.

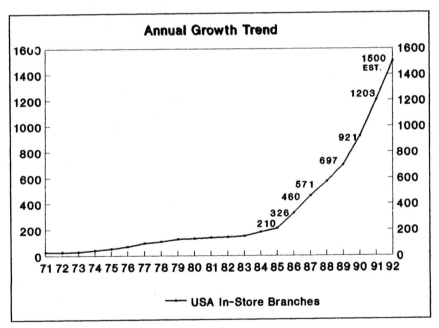

Figure 10–3. Supermarket in-store branches in the United States, 1971–1992. *Source:* International Banking Technologies.

No less a prognosticator than John Naisbitt, author of *Megatrends*, noted in a June 1989 edition of *Trend Letter* that "Grocery stores are emerging as natural sites for branch banking. Watch for similar arrangements between banks and stores to crop up across the U.S. and abroad. It's all part of two trends—synergy and convenience—reshaping the financial services and retailing industries."

"In-store banks, which some customers considered 'a nice touch' when they first opened, will become an essential component of a successful supermarket," predicts Thomas M. Garrott, president of National Commerce Bankcorporation of Memphis, Tennessee.

Garrott speaks with authority. Before joining the Memphis bank in 1982, he had a 17-year career with grocery giant Malone & Hyde, where he worked his way up from division manager to executive vice president for finance and administration. Garrott was asked to join NCBC by chairman and CEO Bruce Campbell to help expand the bank's scope beyond the commercial sector. Campbell chose Garrott because he wasn't a banker, and he had great business skills coupled with a strong retail perspective. Seeing other banks dipping into the supermarket branch concept, Campbell and Garrott decided they had as much expertise, if not more, than anyone else and gave it a try. Most importantly, they saw it as a way to increase their retail business in a very cost-effective way.

Since 1985, NCBC has opened 33 company-owned Super Money Market branches. They've also achieved superstar status among their peers, with a return on equity than rarely dips below 18 percent and a return on assets that exceeds 1.35.

In addition to its own supermarket branches, NCBC offers its expertise to other financial institutions wishing to set up their own versions. Clients can obtain licensing agreements for NCBC's Super Money Market branches, which includes facility design assistance, management support, personnel training, incentive and performance packaging, and operations and marketing help. In 1989 and 1990, such agreements were reached with a diverse geographical selection of financial institutions, including Detroit's Comerica, Inc., Houston's First City Bancorporation, Omaha's FirsTier Financial, Appleton, Wisconsin's Valley Bancorporation, and San Francisco's Wells Fargo Bank.

With 600 traditional branches and over $52 billion in assets, Wells Fargo was one of the first banks to open up the huge California retail market. Wells Fargo joined forces with Safeway, the nation's third largest grocery chain with a quarter of its almost 900 stores in Northern California. In October 1990, Wells Fargo opened their first in-store branch in Vallego, CA. Five more were added within the year, with plans for more in the future. In addition to offering longer weekday hours than traditional offices, the in-store locations are open on Sundays, which research by Safeway has shown to be their second or third busiest day of the week.

Other banks have reported similar growth and success with supermarket locations. According to the *American Banker*, the Seattle-based Olympics Savings Bank added $28 million in deposits and opened more than 13,000 accounts in their 17 branches located in Safeway supermarkets. Cincinnati-based Fifth Third Bancorp has 20 branches in Finast supermarkets in northeastern Ohio and Kroger stores in Ohio, Kentucky and Indiana. In October 1990, the *Wall Street Journal* reported that Pittsburgh's Mellon Bank, once known as "the Morgan of the Alleghenys," opened its first full-service minibank at a Giant Eagle grocery store. "Bankers dressed in aprons roamed the aisles in search of customers," the *Journal* noted.

Because That's Where the Customers Are

Early experiments in in-store financial services can be credited to brokerage and financial advisory services, such as Dean Witter Reynolds, Inc., which placed branches in other retail outlets and mass merchandise companies like Sears, J.C. Penney, and K-Mart. These ventures failed to live up to expectations, however. According to International Banking Technologies (IBT), a leading provider of supermarket banking services, the reasons lay in less frequent visits to these stores than to supermarkets by customers and the reluctance of customers to undertake such complex personal business as financial planning and securities investments in the uncustomary setting of a mass merchandise store.

Supermarket banking, it appears, has not been derailed by these drawbacks. Surveys indicate that supermarkets attract an average of 15,000 to 25,000 consumers per week and that supermarket consumers average 2.4 visits to the same supermarket each week.

A report in the *Orlando Business Journal* in March 1991 chronicled the success of in-store banking in Central Florida. Early in 1989, Orange Bank opened a site inside a Winn Dixie market. In the same year, Southeast Bank agreed to open 15 branches in Gooding's Supermarkets.

Although initially skeptical, Southeast's vice president and area manager Ronald A. Smith did an about-face. "I was extremely surprised that safe deposit boxes went as quickly as they did," he told the *Journal*. "Even the loan side has taken off. . . . The liability side has been phenomenal. We've tripled what we anticipated as far as deposits go."

Low Overhead, High Traffic

According to IBT, a supermarket branch can be staffed by one manager, two full-time and two part-time employees for an annual payroll that is 70 percent of the cost of an average brick and mortar branch. Design and construction costs for a single supermarket branch, which can be as small as 300 to 500 square feet, are one-tenth to one-fifth as much as a brick and mortar version. You could, given those figures, build as many as five to ten supermarket branches for one traditional venue.

The savings continue. Insurance, taxes, maintenance costs, and utilities have all been shown to be substantially higher for brick and mortar branches than in-store models.

Supermarket bank branches can successfully employ many of the same marketing tactics as the traditional branches, including visually attractive signage, point-of-purchase materials such as posters and stand-up boards, brochures and collateral materials on bank services, outdoor billboards, and a variety of paid advertising channels including television, radio, newspapers, and direct mail (see photo at right).

In addition, bank personnel in a supermarket have access to a resource that the brick and mortar facility usually lacks: consumers who don't have an account with your bank. Direct, personal contact with shoppers is an added dimension to supermarket banking. That means sending an employee out onto the food store floor to interact with customers. Research has shown that, if approached, as many as half of them would switch their accounts to the in-store branch. This may explain why banks like Southeast recorded such a surprising increase in new accounts.

John Garnett, executive vice president of IBT, says that the in-store staff should be sufficient to allow one employee to work the aisles at all times during banking hours. The latter most often coincide with store hours, so that customers have the convenience of making a deposit or cashing a check during evening hours or on weekends. As

an icebreaker, staff members should approach shoppers with a small gift, like a keychain, jar opener, or notepad.

"Three basic questions will set up a closing situation," says Garnet." How often do you shop here? At what financial institution(s) do you presently maintain an account? How often do you go to your present bank? Then it is simply a matter of pointing out that the instore branch can handle all of the individual's financial needs at locations and during hours that are more convenient than other financial institutions. By opening an account the person will save time, effort, and money."

The key to success for this approach is to hire friendly, motivated, enthusiastic, and knowledgeable employees. Be aware, too, that supermarket banking is very demanding. The hustle and bustle of the shopping environment puts more strain on employees than the conventional banking scenario. Burnout rates for supermarket banking staff have been recorded at twice the normal rate for brick and mortar employees.

Taking It to the Streets, the Malls, the Fairs

The move away from brick and mortar branches doesn't stop at the supermarket. Other banks, seeking ways to find new customers, have literally taken their show on the road. First National Bank of Jackson, Tennessee, converted an armored truck into a mobile branch bank in 1990. The mobile bank, with two teller windows on one side, follows a regular schedule of stops at nursing homes, public housing projects, shopping malls, and factories. The unit also tours rural communities."Within three years," bank chairman Ernest Vickers III told Fortune magazine, "mobile banks will be as common as UPS delivery trucks."

First National Bank in Albuquerque adapted a recreational vehicle into a traveling ATM which wheels out to local events such as senior citizens' homes, flea markets, and hot-air ballooning meets. The latter draws as many as 150,000 visitors. Data from the ATM transactions is beamed by microwave radio signals to a receiver atop the bank's downtown Albuquerque office and then downloaded to the central computer.

BANKS WITHOUT WALLS

On July 15, 1987, a slightly different approach to branch banking appeared on the American scene. Actually, you could call Key Bank USA the antithesis of the brick and mortar approach. Other than a home office in Albany, New York, Key Bank was a bank without walls, relying on phone service and the mails to take deposits and open money market, certificate of deposit, and IRA accounts.

Instead of face-to-face selling in the branch environment, Key Bank reached its potential customers through newspaper ads with a coupon and an 800 telephone line for direct and immediate response. The bank also appeared in printed surveys that ranked bank-by-mail operations and listed the institutions' address and/or phone number. Key Bank's market spans the entire country and has depositors from all 50 states. Assets in 1991 were listed at $500 million for 10,000 accounts.

Key Bank has capitalized on its low overhead and offered customers high-yield deposits. All prospect and customer information is maintained on a database that also supports cross-selling and other marketing functions.

In addition to being rate-driven, Key Bank focuses on customer service. All new accounts are opened and mailed out the same day they are received. Account representatives are trained to answer a broad range of questions, from information about the FDIC to questions about the bank's operations. Without the face-to-face factor, the CSRs are responsible for making customers feel comfortable with a bank that they will probably never see.

Key Bank's customer service staff numbers only 17, according to president and CEO Deborah L. Bevier, which is about a tenth of what a brick and morter-based institution of the same size would require. Administration and other staff, including employees who work in their equipment leasing affiliate, total another 71.

"There's a large part of the population who wouldn't bank by mail even if we had the highest rate and were the safest bank in the country," says Bevier. "Nevertheless, I'm watching my 18-year-old son grow up and I see that there just aren't the same ties or the same loyalties to the local community. We're one of the few who've specialized in this kind of banking, but it's a growing niche. Look at the mutual funds, where nearly all transactions are done by phone or through the mail. The time constraints that have been placed on the modern two wage-earner families makes us look for alternative ways to get the services we need easily and conveniently."

Branchless banking has also put down some roots in England, where FirstDirect Bank in Leeds opened its "doors" in October 1989. The brainchild of Midland Bank Plc.'s chairman Sir Kit McMahon, the financial institution conducts all business with customers by phone and never shuts down. A centralized automatic call distributor (ACD) from Datapoint drives the integrated voice processing system, which includes Coffman's Telebusiness EDGE software and Davox voice/data workstations. The bank can handle up to 190 concurrent callers. FirstDirect invested more than five million dollars (U.S.) in the core telebanking system.

FirstDirect employs a staff of about 250. Specially trained personal banking representatives work around the clock. Other product specialists field callers' more complicated questions regarding insurance, brokerate, and other lines of business. FirstDirect customers avail themselves of all the traditional financial products from checking and savings accounts to mortgages, credit cards, and investment products. Since operating costs are significantly lower than branch banking institutions, FirstDirect offers higher rates for savings and lower rates for credit products. Customers use an ATM card to get instant cash on the street.

Leveraging Customer Service with Technology

One of the promises of automation has always been leveraging human effort with technology. Little wonder that the demand to maintain customer service and increase sales while reducing staff, that is, the prevailing ethos of banking for the past several years, has coincided with the interest and increased usage of technology in the banking arena. In addition, the explosion of banking products has placed a strain on qualified service representatives who can answer customers' requests for information and service.

One solution would be to create a delivery system whereby product specialists could be available wherever consumers have banking access. Personal Financial Assistant, Inc. of Charlotte, North Carolina has developed the Automated Service Machine (ASM) to provide a solution, an idea that has fallen on fertile ground at a few banks, notably Banc One Corp. and Huntington Bancshares, both in Columbus, Ohio, and Crossland Savings Bank in New York.

Introduced in 1991, the ASM can handle as many as 400 products, including installment loans, mortgages, investments, and insurance policies. The 13.5 foot high, 550 pound unit also requires no human on-site staff. Unlike an ATM, the ASM is portable and takes only two hours to assemble. The communication hookup requires two standard jacks and a pair of regular phone lines. (See photo at right.)

To use the ASM, a customer enters the ASM and picks up the telephone. There are no computer keys to operate, which should encourage those consumers who find themselves PC-illiterate or computer-phobic. By simply pushing a button, the customer is connected to a live CSR whose image appears on the television screen.

While the person visiting the kiosk can see the CSR, the reverse is not true. The banker hears only the customer's voice. This faceless interaction guarantees nondiscrimination based on appearance. "It doesn't discriminate," PFA president Richard D'Agostino told *USA Today* in August 1991. "I'm going to get the loan or not based on my good record, whether I come in in rags or a $900 suit."

Based on the customer's inquiry, the CSR selects from the product menu. Information about the desired product is presented simultaneously to both parties. Product proposals, illustrations, and loan quotations can all be printed out on-site by a laser printer included in the ASM. The CSR prepares the application and sends a copy, again via the laser printer, to the customer for his or her signature. They then leave one copy in the security box and take the other for their records.

TECHNOLOGY THAT BREAKS THROUGH BARRIERS

Is There an Expert in the House?

Of all the technologies to emerge from the 1980s, a decade of computer-related explosion in the financial industry, few have a more provocative moniker than "expert systems." A branch of artificial intelligence, expert systems attempt to marry the fruits of human knowledge with the calculating powers of the computer. The result, if engineered correctly, provides financial service employees with a "smart" tool with which they can analyze, monitor, authorize, and perform other applications. Ideally, these functions can be carried out with both improved decision-making quality and increased staff productivity.

Basically, expert systems are built by transforming the rules and judgments used by experts in areas such as mortgage lending or credit authorization into software code. Early attempts at the process involved a deductive reasoning approach, but more recently the focus has shifted to inductive reasoning. The former relied on a series of if/then assumptions that required exhaustive programming.

The inductive version, on the other hand, takes a representative group of situations and creates a basic set of rules. As more cases are run through the program, it will "teach" itself and expand the knowledge base. Software makers point out that the the inductive approach works best for a pragmatic expert, someone like a loan officer who has been doing loans for a while and often goes by his or her gut feeling.

Expert systems have found favorable terrain in the loan review arena. Cogensys, a software company based in La Jolla, CA, developed a package called Judgement Processor. In May 1990, B. F. Saul, the mortgage underwriting subsidiary of Chevy Chase Federal Savings Bank in Chevy Chase, Virginia, launched "MortgageVision." The internally developed product utilized Judgement Processor to create a system that reduces the loan application and commitment process from two weeks down to less than half an hour.

B. F. Saul's loan officers gather data on their laptop PCs and send the information via modem to the bank's mainframe, which pulls in the required data from credit bureaus and mortgage insurers. The mortgage underwriters are likewise linked via a local area network (LAN). Once the consumer information and credit reports have been captured, the underwriter sends the information to the expert system. Judgement Processor has been taught by the bank's staff to make a decision in each of 14 areas. It then makes a recommendation based on those answers and points out potential problems with the loan. The information is then routed back to the underwriter, who makes the final call.

Easy to install, Judgement Processor continues to improve at emulating the decisions that the bank's best loan officers would make. A senior bank officer compares it to "one of those heuristic chess games that learns through experience."

By capturing the reasoning and logic of the bank's best minds, expert systems become excellent teaching tools as well. For example, as older loan officers retire, their wisdom is passed on to the next generation, as well as providing a safety net in the decision-making process.

Banks have trailed behind the securities and insurance industries in developing expert systems, but that situation has begun to change. Basic criteria for applying an expert system in different financial situations have emerged. In general, such a system can be most useful when there is a problem or decision that

- Requires complex logic
- Calls for judgements or rules of thumb
- Is based on uncertain or incomplete information
- Evaluates multiple or hypothetical solutions

Preserving a Corporate Asset—Knowledge

Expert systems also make sense in areas where expertise is expensive or scarce. That's one of the major reasons that prompted Cincinnati's Star Bank to employ an expert system for its $100 million credit card portfolio. The move grew out of their inability to locate qualified credit analysts. Bank management also wanted consistency and a system that could handle large volumes.

Star Bank, which acts as the flagship for Star Bank Corporation's 16 member banks in Ohio, Indiana, and Kentucky, chose an experienced credit analyst to mentor the software. He fed thousands of examples into the database before putting the system into production early in 1990. Both approvals and denials were monitored to assure quality. In addition, the bank built an electronic link to their bank customer information file to automatically look for deposit information that might influence their decision.

In addition to credit and loan analyses, expert systems have found their way into other areas. Personal financial advisor systems counsel customers on investment products. Real estate appraisal programs review the status of properties owned by banks. Expert systems assist in funds transfers as well as foreign exchange trading and monitoring.

Also important is the size of the application for which the expert system is to be implemented. A trivial situation won't justify the effort, and something too complex may never get finished. The Arthur D. Little Center of Financial Research and Development in Cambridge, MA, warns that bank staff will lose interest if the project takes too long. "We like to demonstrate the system's capability within 90 days and have it in production within six months," said the Center's director Robert Moll.

That doesn't mean that big problems can't be successfully addressed. England's Trustee Savings Bank used an expert system to develop a computer-based training program for 25,000 employees across 1,250 branches. Developed on high-powered workstations, the KES program, a product of Software Architecture & Engineering in Arlington, Virginia, trained bank employees to sell and promote debit cards.

Trustee Savings Bank officials estimate that the program would have taken months, if not years, to develop using conventional programming methods. Instead, the process took eight weeks. As a result, the bank was able to quickly and efficiently train its staff at an estimated cost of only $2 to $3 per employee.

There are also gains to be made by imbedding small expert systems into the day-to-day operations such as helping explain products or banking terminology to customers. Generally, there is one person in the bank who can do the latter better than anyone else. If you can replicate them with an expert system, you'll improve the quality of service throughout the bank. Industry experts list productivity gains— by as much as 30 to 35 percent—and improved quality of service as the main benefits to be accessed by the use of expert systems.

Oak Hills Savings and Loan in Cincinnati, Ohio recently added an expert system to their account processing system to help eliminate errors when changes were made to the bank's Standard Account Type Table (SATT). The SATT controls how the customers' accounts are processed at the institution's third party data center.

In this case, the expert system replaced a hardbound paper manual, which had been used to generate paper requests to alter the existing SATT configuration or develop additional ones for new products. Under the old system, the person making the request didn't always notice that the changes for which they were asking required other modifications in the SATT configuration. The expert system electronically notices inconsistencies and diagnoses a solution. It also cuts the time required for the change from a week to as short as a day.

Focusing on the Ends, Not the Means

Some caveats exist for those considering the use of expert systems. One is not to become vendor driven. "Institutions that don't appreciate their own level of expertise will be exposed to 'shrink wrapped' systems, where you're buying someone else's knowledge," according to Arthur Little's Robert Moll. "You just don't know if it's good for you."

Likewise, expert systems should be treated as a tool, not an ultimate solution. Applications often involve nonexpert system aspects, and the entire package has to be integrated. Financial services industry consultant Bob Friedenberg of Inference Corporation stresses the importance of aligning the various departments that will be involved. They include

- Management information systems people who will support the project and supply the data
- Experts who'll give you the rules framework
- End users, who may differ from the experts
- Functional management, who can incorporate management policies and procedures into the system as it's being built

Other areas to consider are how long the process will take, the degree of difficulty in building a system and its effect on the bottom line, and whether you'll be running the system on a mainframe, PCs, networks, or a combination of hardware configurations. Pick the appropriate platform. A highly interactive expert system that requires constant feedback might work best on a PC or a LAN network. Systems that monitor information that can be run in batches might work better on a mainframe. Transferring existing data is another issue to consider. You want to be able to access your data without taking up additional storage space in the expert system.

SWIFT AND SURE COMMUNICATION NETWORKS

Technology can be, and has also been, applied to the operations side of modern banking, with favorable and, in some cases, considerable impact on the bottom line. Those bankers who haven't considered these applications need to reconsider their priorities and the opportunities to improve their profitability.

Electronic communications offer speed and efficiency, promising better service to customers. Many bankers are already familiar with elements of electronic banking, such as the automated clearing house (ACH), which was developed by the Federal Reserve and the banking industry in the late 1960s. ACH's growth has been held in check by several factors, including complex formats, loss of float issues, and lack of consumer education. Those involved with ACH have remained optimistic, however, noting that customers who use the service to direct-deposit their paychecks tend to keep higher balances in their accounts.

"We're trying to make it easier to bank with us," said a manager of telecommunications for a major Southeast bank. "The best banks of the future are the ones that will offer better service. We need to know more about the customer, and that information has to be able to follow the customer from branch to branch. You can store that data at a central site, but how do you move it back and forth quickly?"

The recent upsurge in mergers, which have produced megabanks and superregionals, accentuates the need to move customer data quickly and efficiently. Building communication networks to store, process, and report those data has become a critical element in the bank's overall well-being.

Support of this statement comes from a survey conducted by Motorola Codex of Mansfield, Massachusetts, of 21 major financial institutions across the country, including Chase Manhattan, Citicorp, Manufacturers Hanover, Sanwa of California, and Bank of America. Those polled represented, at the time, 22% of the total assets of banks and S&Ls in the U.S.

"They believe that electronic networks are the mechanism for them to be competitive and to get information out to the end user, whether it's their employees or the customers themselves," said Toni Waeghe, a former banker with Chase Manhattan who helped compile the study for Codex, a data communication systems company. "If they can do that faster and better than anyone else, then they'll keep their market share."

Consolidating a bank's multiple elements is one of the first issues to address. Technology consultants like to talk about high-speed digital "backbones" made up of T-1 lines. A T-1 facility digitally transmits up to 1.544 million bits of voice, data, or video information per second. T-1 offers several advantages over traditional phone line service. By consolidating 24 channels, or circuits, into a single line, the service cuts communication costs and gives the user more flexibility to keep up with changes and add new services quickly. In addition, T-1 transmissions offer higher quality than traditional analog communications.

In 1989, Security Pacific Bank in Los Angeles completed installation of an extensive T-1 network after an aggressive expansion through acquisitions. The bank needed to tie together data centers from Southern California to Seattle on the West Coast and east to New York, as well as overseas. Once installed, the network processed 7 million checks a day from over 600 branches and 1,300 ATMs, in addition to the bank's 25,000 phone sets. The head of the bank's network and computer services referred to the system as a "computer utility," and compared it to gas and electricity. "The bank staff and customers don't care where the data service comes from," he said, "just that it's there when they need it."

Of course, not all banks can match the transmitting requirements or telecommunication budgets of giants like Security Pacific (or its recent acquirer, Bank of America). Fractional T-1 service, by which banks can buy a portion of a network for their communication needs, is available. In addition to voice and data demands, this partial service suits video transmissions for face-to-face conferencing.

Reaching for the Stars

Not all banks have limited themselves to ground transmissions. **First Union Bank** pioneered the use of satellite communications, a path that others, such as Barnett Banks of Jacksonville, Florida, and Chase Manhattan Bank in New York, have also chosen to follow.

(Continued)

In 1988, First Union began installing very small aperture terminals (VSATs) atop its branches in the Southeast. The devices beam signals over 22,000 miles into space where a satellite reflects them back to bank headquarters in Charlotte. During an ATM transaction, for example, the signal triggers a check of the customer's account and returns the OK or denial for issuing cash. From start to finish, the process takes only three seconds. The VSATs also support branch automation, account inquiries, and employee computer-based training throughout First Union's 800 branches.

By going to outer space, First Union has bypassed the delays and frustrations that often accompany the installation and repair of land-based lines. In addition, by controlling their communication network, the bank predicts a savings of more than $1 million a year from 1990 to 1995.

Perhaps the most dramatic advantage First Union gained with their VSAT system was their ability to weather the devastating Hurricane Hugo of 1989 with a minimum of downtime. None of the bank's VSAT 1.8-meter antennas were damaged by the 130 mph winds that slammed into the Carolinas. While other banks had to wait for telephone repairs, First Union was able to go back online as soon as electrical power resumed.

At the end of 1989, Chase Manhattan also joined the VSAT ranks, installing a terminal at their Mexico City office. The system beams voice and data back and forth to a network hub in Dallas, which is connected to New York by fiber-optic cable. Citing a $3,000 monthly savings in their telecommunications bill, the bank also noted that the satellite approach bypasses unreliable local telephone systems, a problem not uncommon in lesser developed nations.

Branching off the digital backbone are smaller communication lines to various bank functions such as teller terminals, ATMs, and administrative offices. The devices used to collect information from these various sources, or to disperse it on the receiving end, are called multiplexers.

Perle Systems' OneLine and Paradyne's Banking Modem are two examples of multiplexers, designed to merge networks onto a single telephone line. Fractional T-1 multiplexers are also available, such as Timeplex's LINK products. "The breakup of AT&T and the resulting deregulation of phone service increased the importance of communication for banks," according to Perle's Scott Forler, adding that the

OneLine multiplexer is appropriate for banks with 20 or more branches and five or more ATMs. Using it to combine input from ATMs, teller terminals, and platform automation systems can pay for itself within 18 months to two years.

Back-ups are an integral part of any electronic communication system. Perle's OneLine features automatic recovery software that kicks in if the primary system goes down. The system also has an intercept switch connecting the bank's ATM to a regional or national network, such as Cirrus or MAC, which will operate the ATM if the bank's main computer goes offline or breaks down.

Once the data have made their way from the field, software becomes the critical factor in being able to read the information. Shared Financial Systems (SFS) of Dallas, Texas, specializes in software that allows banks to tie into and/or tie together various computers, ATMs, and other systems. SFS's core software, which actually completes the transactions, exists inside a "shell" of translation code that interprets the data. New or different devices, which may result from bank mergers or the utilization of devices like mobile branches, can thus be folded into the bank's system without having to rewrite the core software.

11

Productivity and Profitability

Compared to other industry sectors, banking and financial industry have long led in technology expenditures. There is no evidence, however, that those expenditures have led to increased productivity. This is one-half of the bane of existence of bank CEOs.

The other half is profit-pressures. The industry average return on assets (ROA) of .7 is just not good enough. Which change-masters, bank managers of money and machinery, will lead the charge to greater productivity and profitability in the 1990s?

PRODUCTIVITY: THE ELUSIVE GOAL

The High and Mighty Efficient

A 1989 survey by Anderson Consulting of 70 American banks with assets ranging from $2 to $30 billion revealed some intriguing data on productivity. A quarter of those institutions, which represented a majority of all regional banks, did not even collect productivity information! Conversely, the survey found that an important strategy of the high-productivity banks was tracking key productivity measures. Those institutions that don't know how they're doing are like the young children who hope that, by covering their eyes, they won't be afraid of the danger around them.

The survey also illuminated other boondoggles and dark secrets. For one, low productivity has a multiplier effect and can make as much as a fourfold difference in the productivity of employees across all areas of a bank. Size, although it gives larger banks an advantage in achieving economies of scale, is not an overriding factor. However, through *centralization* and *standardization* of noncustomer functions, such as administration and operations, smaller banks can achieve operating economies and genuinely improve productivity.

High productivity also does not mean instituting great numbers of programs to achieve that end. By focusing resources on a smaller range of strategies that target particular goals, high-performing banks enjoy greater success.

Centralization and standardization do not translate ipso facto to automation, even though the latter can play an important role. The Arthur Anderson consultants involved with the survey don't believe the paperless office is "around the corner," however. Of equal if not greater importance is the issue of worker productivity, especially in the area of human resource management. Helping people work smarter, to which automation can contribute, is crucial to the future success of an organization.

To underscore the last point, consider the disclosure by the Federal Deposit Insurance Corporation in June 1990 that accounting errors at some savings and loans were going to potentially cost the agency some $8 billion! These faulty overcharges were partly the result of bad calculations made by underpaid high-school graduates who were often hired to service those loans. Cutting costs in the wrong place, that is, in human resources, can be much more expensive in the long run.

Consolidating Back from the Brink

Perhaps the most dramatic bank recovery in recent memory was that negotiated by San Francisco's Bank of America in the 1980s. Founded in 1904 by a former produce manager, the charismatic A. P. Giannini, the once robust institution fell on hard times during the first half of the decade. Samuel Armacost, successor to the legendary CEO A.W. Clausen, ran into a snake's pit of problems after taking the helm in 1981. Not the least of those was a sprawling operation that had resulted from the bank's growth spurt in the 1970s.

Although he will most likely be footnoted in history as the banker who almost crashed BofA on the rocky shore of financial ruin, Armacost did recognize that one of the keys to increasing productivity would be the consolidation of bank functions. One of his positive legacies has been BankAmerica Systems Engineering, or BASE, which was launched in January 1985, to centralize and standardize the bank's systems and data processing departments.

Being held responsible for a 1984 Top 10 U.S. banking rating better only than the one for stricken Continental Illinois, Armacost should also receive some acknowledgment for committing a $5 billion budget to BASE. He recognized that consolidation was needed in order to unravel the spaghetti system of 60 worldwide networks that transported and delivered information and services to the inefficient mass that BofA had become.

Most bank technologists, even if they aren't facing the magnitude of problems that beset BofA at the time, can relate to the three levels of the problem that BASE addressed:

- Maintaining old systems and expanding them to keep up with the marketplace and new regulations
- Integrating old and new systems, often ones that were not meant for such a marriage
- Creating a new open-end system that could accept new products and direction without disruptions

A soul-searching self-examination revealed that the bank's systems had previously been *product-oriented*. Individual groups, such as retail or loan operations, had built or found solutions that met their particular needs. However, there had been little emphasis on centralized servicing for customers, who often experienced frustration as they were routed from one department to another in search of account or transaction information. This approach created the image of the bank as insensitive, which was an undesired public persona for a bank with over 870 branch offices in the Golden State.

Ground-Up Solutions

The foundation for the solution was to create a horizontally layered applications architecture. The database comprised the bottom layer.

Over it lay the orchestrating or dispatching strata, which organized data from the bottom layer and sent it through to the top layer. The latter was comprised of the bank's delivery points, including ATMs, customer service terminals, and teller terminals.

Part of the centralization process included concentrating BofA's data centers into key locations. Bank management felt that a small number of large centers would be more cost effective. The rent was cheaper than a large number of small centers and they achieved economy of scale and standardization. They could also focus their considerable computing power in those centers to handle the large volumes.

Concurrently, the bank streamlined communications with its proprietary California Data Network. T-1 lines connected the three major data centers in San Francisco, Los Angeles, and Concord, California. These were in turn linked to nine backbone access sites. Fanning out from these were 100 service area centers, each of which connected with at least two access sites for redundancy. The final stop on the communication loop was the individual branches.

From the retail perspective, BofA's consolidation was seen as critical to providing the delivery mechanisms to get the cost structure right. "Our margins are getting thinner and thinner," said an executive in the California Banking Division. "We shouldn't be talking to other banks, because they're just as stupid as we are. We should be talking to Macy's, Nordstrom, and Safeway. They're retailers and so are we. They've figured out how to match resources to volume, how to do the right cost equation evaluations and how to match up revenues."

Perhaps BofA's consolidation efforts were best exemplified by its introduction of *Alpha*—an all-in-one checking and savings account with an overdraft line of credit. The move also emphasized BofA's shift from its previous focus on international lending to the retail basis upon which Giannini originally built his empire. Benefitting from a tremendous marketing push, Alpha pulled in over 350,000 accounts during the first six months of operation. Industry sources estimate that about 40 percent of those were new to the bank.

Alpha was not, however, a terribly complicated or even revolutionary product, but one that combined separate elements already present in the bank. Richard Rosenberg, who headed BofA's retail division at the time and became CEO of the bank in 1990, had created one of the first such packaged accounts while working for rival Wells Fargo

Bank in 1973. BofA didn't even build a new system for Alpha. Instead, they modified a half-dozen stable, existing ones and pulled in elements from up to 40 others.

The success of *Alpha* and other measures, including a massive reduction in staff, resulted in one of banking's greatest turnarounds. After losing almost $1.8 billion in 1986 and 1987 and canceling shareholder's dividends, BofA announced yearly earnings for 1988 of $726 million. The bank's stock price tripled and quarterly dividends were restored. While much of the rebound was publicly credited to the return of A. W. Clausen, bank insiders knew there were additional factors involved. "The quality of our computer services kept us going and have been a key element in getting us out of our problems," said the vice president in charge of operations for BASE.

BofA's return to health was so dramatic that the institution went from being in danger of being acquired to an aggressive acquirer, gobbling up banks in the western United States, including Hawaii, Texas, Arizona, New Mexico, Oregon, Utah, and Nevada, not to mention a merger with intrastate rival Security Pacific. The latter, still pending approval at press time, would nearly double BofA's asset size from $118 to $190 billion and solidifying its position behind Citicorp as the nation's second largest bank. On the eve of the relaxation of California's interstate banking regulations, the behemoth superregional was poised to fulfill founder Giannini's original dream of branches from coast to coast. BofA made a strong bid for the faltering Bank of New England when the eastern superregional came into play in 1991.

Centralizing for Increased Efficiency

The bank that beat out BofA for the Bank of New England was the smaller, yet very efficient, Fleet/Norstar Financial Group of Providence, Rhode Island. The merger coup, announced in April 1991, moved Fleet/Norstar from 20th on the U.S. banking scale to 12th, and firmly established the 200-year-old bank as the dominant player in New England and upstate New York.

Praise for Fleet/Norstar as a strong performer was nearly unanimous from the research departments of Salomon Brothers, Merrill Lynch, Goldman Sachs, and Montgomery Securities. Frequently mentioned in their analyses was the bank's demonstrated ability to handle consolidation and its superiority as "one of the lowest-cost

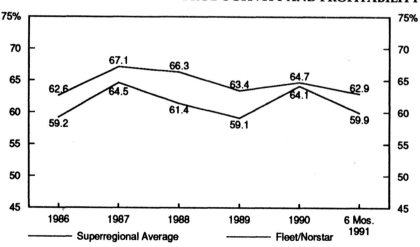

Figure 11–1.   Salomon's overhead ratio graph.

servicers in the industry." Despite their presence in the poor real-estate loan market of the Northeast, Fleet/Norstar has, according to Salomon Brothers, maintained an overhead ratio (comparing expenses to total revenues) below that of the supperregional bank composite for the past five years (see Figure 11–1).

Salomon Brothers also predicted that after an 18-month transition period during which the Bank of New England operations would be folded into Fleet/Norstar, the bank would recognize "dramatic cost savings of up to $350 million per year." Among the key areas from which these savings would flow was systems and support, accounting for some $90 million in reduced costs.

Masterful Mergery

Centralization and standardization have been bread and butter issues at Fleet/Norstar since 1987 when two separate and somewhat equal institutions, Fleet Financial Group and Norstar Bancorp, merged eight banks and 16 nonbank financial services companies. Mastermind of the data processing and bank operations consolidation was Mike Zucchini, CEO of Fleet/Norstar Services Company and CIO of Fleet/Norstar Financial Group. In a 1989 Harvard Business School case study, Zucchini said that he "didn't see this job as purely data processing and back room operations." He continued, "I see it as giving customers access to information and service. We've spent this year talking about savings. What I want people talking about next year is our ability to compete in the marketplace." The Bank of New England merger certainly bore out his words.

Fleet/Norstar management adopted a matrix system whereby subsidiary presidents took on vertical responsibilities while at the same time certain corporate officers' authority extended horizontally through various subsidiaries with specific responsibilities. This bidirectional management system requires open communication, but has resulted in a highly energized and efficient banking operation.

The challenge was combining two distinct and entrenched technology bases. Fleet had been active in commercial banking in the Northeast and nonbanking activities nationwide, and had spent its time on strategies for product development. Norstar had focused on community banking. Between 1972 and 1988, the institution had bought 34 banks or groups of branches, and had concentrated on consolidating and fine-tuning those acquisitions.

On the operations level, Fleet's data processing staff numbered 400, while Norstar had half as many employees in the same area. Both banks used IBM's MVS/XA operating system, but class structures, naming conventions, and utility software differed. Hardware differences existed as well, such as Norstar's use of self-loading cartridge disks versus Fleet's older sysem of hand-loaded tapes with higher data error rates.

Banking consultants constantly preach about the importance of getting senior management involved and committed in any changes planned for a financial institution's operating procedures. That point was dramatically illustrated in the Fleet/Norstar consolidation process. When J. Terrence Murray, who had moved from CEO of Fleet to the same position in Fleet/Norstar, was told at a January, 1988, board meeting that Zucchini was being kept "informed" of progress in merging data centers, he retorted: "I don't want him just informed. I want him to be responsible." This forceful annunciation bestowed upon Zucchini the genuine authority he needed to implement his program.

Zucchini brainstormed with top-level data-processing staff from the different geographical areas and they emerged with a plan to concentrate operations in one center. By combining this move with the introduction of a single set of applications software, Zucchini outlined plans to save $10 million out of the 1988 data-processing budget of over $55 million (a promise which he effectively delivered).

Albany, New York was chosen as data center site, partially because of more favorable tax considerations. During a six-month changeover period, the bank ran parallel computer processing in both Providence, their old site, and upstate New York. By May 1989, the transition had been completed.

Creating singular applications software was designed to minimize data processing and support costs and, at the same time, take advantage of economies of scale. Strategically, the bank builds products at one site, a move that consolidates time and effort. More attention can then be put into putting procedures into place and making sure they work correctly.

The establishment of a services company includes charging back bank operations and data processing costs to individual banks. This program encourages common solutions and efficient use of information systems recourse. Changes and modifications are handled by committee, which tends to bring issues out in the open that otherwise might get buried in individual banks or corporate departments. On the other hand, local bankers can still define their own products through system parameters in regards to products names, service charges, terms, and interest rates. Maintaining the fine balance between centralized control and local autonomy can be difficult at times, but Fleet/Norwest has shown that the benefits are worth the effort.

For BofA, Fleet/Norstar, and other banks seeking to increase their market share, maintaining profitability plays a critical role as their operations continue to grow. A key element in the realization of their intentions will be the technology foundations upon which to build their success, whether local, regional, or national.

SYSTEMS SUPPORT SUCCESS

Analyzing for Profitability

It would be hard to argue against the notion that automation has laid the groundwork for increased employee productivity. Those who make and sell ever-increasingly powerful processing systems and other automation tools constantly trumpet this advantage. Yet, like any change to an organic system, the introduction of these factors affects other routines and work flow patterns. Modifications are needed

PC-Charged Performance

One product designed specifically to address these issues is the *Branch Analyzer* from Earnings Performance Group. The PC-based system tracks and analyzes the performance of the retail network of a bank, including operational efficiency, customer service, fee income, operating costs, staff retention, market share, and cross-selling.

Branch Analyzer retains all appropriate information as a time series and understands how these data should be handled in calculations and graphic displays. Data are organized into logical homogeneous groups, even when the sources for these data originate in diverse systems. The presentation of data is layered, allowing the viewer to break out summary values to obtain additional detail along several different dimensions.

Branch Analyzer also features an annotation feature. Data elements, rows, columns, or whole screens of information can be tagged either permanently or for a specific lifetime. All notes may be grouped into multiple families so that all references to a particular annotation can be identified.

The system assumes that users will want to look at things the designers did not envision. The *Branch Analyzer* database lets the user know which data elements are of particular interest, as well as rating them and determining their affect on other factors. Together, these features allow the user to create ad hoc exception criteria and prioritize their impact on the key parameters driving the corporation.

Some examples of areas for monitoring include

- Deposit growth month to month for five primary deposit products
- Net deposit account growth for the same five products
- Number of new loans booked for four critical loan periods
- Trends related to paid employee hours compared to teller transaction volume and platform product, sales and inquiry volume
- Fee income trends for critical products, including NSF/OD charges, service charges, money orders and cashier's checks, and loan origination fees
- Operating expense trends for those expense categories which can be controlled at the branch level.

to fully implement the benefits from technology. Procedures must be revised. New and different skills must be developed. Better scheduling must be put in place.

Historically, banks have been among the heaviest users of data processing. Utilizing the data collected, stored, processed, and reported daily, however, has yet to be exploited in many cases. Among the problems inherent in this glut of data are the lack of any perspective of trends through time, the difficulty in obtaining cross-application exception reporting, and the lack of ability to pinpoint problem areas down to specific departments and/or managers.

Busting Productivity Gaps

Productivity analyses, performed either internally or by an outside vendor, can unearth ways in which to put some of those automation advantages to work. These studies, when undertaken with an honest intent to discover new solutions and answer long-standing questions, offer an objective view of your operations. They can provide a snapshot of individual areas of concern or institutionwide issues.

Examples of productivity analyses abound. Here are a few:

When analysts from Electronic Data Systems (EDS) surveyed procedures at the 44 branch Sacramento Savings and Loan, they found enough in their review to create a 90-point recommended action plan. When implemented, the changes resulted in an annual savings of nearly $550,000.

In the loan-processing area, for example, the team found that the institution's staff was not taking advantage of their "smart teller" terminals. These expensive and sophisticated machines, designed to post payments, were instead being used for inquiries or maintaining files. Those lower level functions could just as easily be performed on less costly dumb terminals.

The EDS team also found that certain transactions took inordinately long to complete because tellers had to search for information located on different computer screens. The solution was to employ customized screens that could pull information from different sources and display the results all at once. Average transaction times were reduced, as well as giving operators the ability to process multiple transactions automatically.

Since 1989, employees at Norwest Bank in Minneapolis/St. Paul, Minnesota have been coming up with money-saving and productivity-enhancing ideas under a program known as "Gapbusters." Designed to reduce the "gaps between what our customers expect and what we deliver," according to a bank spokesperson, Gapbusters offers cash prizes up to $5,000 for new ways to improve service.

Winners of the 1990 top prize were members of the bank's Delivery Support's Systems Team in North Dakota. The lengthy amount of time it was taking employees to retrieve customer information by switching from one computer program to another prompted the search for an easier solution. The systems team devised a way to cut the number of steps in half by simply entering a few simple command lines. Not only did this method save time and improve service delivery, but it also rescued the bank from up to $250,000 in additional development costs that would have been required to improve the software.

At the Branch Banking & Trust Co. (BB&T) in Wilson, North Carolina, management had been trying to alter the spending ethos in order to impact the bottom line through financial responsibility. Wherever possible, invoices were charged back to the person or area of the bank that generated them. This approach worked on the principle that, if the departments knew they would be responsible for the whole amount, they would think twice about placing the order.

At the bank's central purchasing house for bank forms and supplies, for example, inventoried items were billed out to different areas as they ordered, just as if they bought the supplies from a retailer. Bank management took the attitude that the decision-makers have to face the financial consequences just as if they were running their own business.

The bank's phone system was also affected. Formerly, branches could call into bank headquarters on an 800 WATS toll-free line. That method provided no way of tracing individual calls, a job that could only be accomplished manually. BB&T switched to MCI's Virtual Network system, which created a separate network for the bank at a lower cost and everyone who makes a call is billed separately, just like a regular phone service. Under this program, those branches that make many calls get charged accordingly.

Profitability and Customer Relationships

In addressing attendees at the 1988 National Operations and Automation Conference (NOAC), banking consultant John Owens Jr. discussed the concept of measuring customer relationship profitability. Owens argued, "We bankers must obtain a better handle on pricing for profitability, both in our products and relationships. But this must be done within the context of your target markets—their needs, priorities, and preferences. . . ."

Profitability analysis, Owens also noted, measures the entire relationship with the customer, including assets, liabilities, and services used. It must also establish accountability for the creation and maintenance of those profitable relationships. Potential users must choose which system. Among the most frequently used are

- Gross yield on net funds used
- Net yield on net funds used
- Net yield on loans
- Net margin on total revenue
- Net yield on capital

Equally important as the system chosen is the establishment of standards by which to compare results of the analysis, using either a desired, median, or benchmark yield. Each will work, but all parties must be in agreement as to which they'll use.

Characteristically, those banks that succeed at these functions tend to be more competitive in their marketplace, to target specific markets and customers more intelligently, and to allocate the proper resources to optimize fee income.

THE ROCKY ROAD OF RISK MANAGEMENT

More than 50 companies offer models and systems for profitability analysis. That broad spectrum can make bank managers feel not unlike new car buyers surveying the showroom floor. Standard software provides basic transporation. Sporty, intermediate models offer lots of optional modules. At the upper end, supercharged, sophisticated, decision-support systems enable large institutions and super-regionals to manage multidimensional risks in complex courses of retail, as well as wholesale and international, banking.

Spreads between assets and liabilities, even with the increased attention to income from fees, trading, and other sources, still determine the health of today's banks. And while asset liability management (ALM) was once only the main concern of a bank's asset/ liability management committee (ALCO), others have become interested in the process. Primary among the latter group are the Federal regulators, who are requiring higher capital ratios and more conservative asset valuations. The Feds hope that by getting a clearer ALM picture of banks, they can prevent another savings and loan fiasco.

The fast (some might call it reckless) growth of the 1980s has caused many banks to slow down their real estate and commercial lending operations, particularly in depressed economic areas. Some have been forced into used asset sales to improve their capital ratios. Other institutions caught up in the race have lost sight of their purpose and destination, traveling aimlessly in circles.

Turbocharged systems and glitzy ALM software programs won't, by themselves, produce winning performance. ALM systems can, however, act as the engines that drive successful bank management strategies. In the words of George K. Darling, president of the Darling Consulting Group in Newburyport, Massachusetts, these systems can "develop and support ALM processes to maximize net income within acceptable levels of interest rate risk and liquidity risk while maintaining adequate capital levels."

Interest-rate forces and a constricting economy have challenged ALCOs to mitigate their risk exposure in new ways. ALM systems and ALCOs serve many masters, including the regulators, boards of directors, stockholders and analysts, and bank's top management.

Back to Basics

In working with numerous clients, Darling has seen a growing trend away from theory and toward the fundamental basics. "If a banker cannot understand analytical tools and formulas to explain them to the board, he won't use them," he said.

The three main elements of any ALM strategy, according to Darling, are *credit risk, interest rate risk,* and *liquidity risk.* Most ALM systems can handle interest rate risk management and budgeting basics with few problems. Before the gyrations caused by deregulation in the 1980s, deposits supported the lending activity of banks. ALCOs concentrated on predicting future conditions and incorporating those changes into the balance sheet.

Hard times in the commercial and real estate portfolios has increased the focus on credit risk. Likewise, liquidity risk has become an area of heightened concern. David Gilbert, senior vice president and director of financial industry consulting at Logica Data Architects in Waltham, Massachusetts, noted that "liquidity management involves developing stable deposit relationships that enable bankers to weather short-term problems. Once bankers get back to basics they can start to develop reasonable parameters and measurement systems to run the balance sheet." Getting back to basics also heralds a return to the fundamentals of banking, the core business(es) of the bank, key financial performance goals such as return on earnings (ROE), and market position and share.

The commercial lending excesses and overdevelopment of the 1980s did not deter Keith Patten, CEO at Camden National Bank, from making new loans in a conservative yet constructive fashion. Headquartered in the midcoast of Maine, Camden National is a case study in high-performance banking. In 1990, return on assets was 1.51 and ROE measured nearly 20 percent. In that year, the state superintendent of banks named Camden National the best bank in Maine in terms of earnings, low percentage of nonperforming loans, and high capital ratio. The bank has pursued stable, sensible growth. From 1982 to the end of 1990, assets grew from $65 million to $283 million.

In many ways, though, Camden National never strayed from the basics. They kept their lending local and raised all their deposits within their market area. The bank employed SunGard Financial System's Balance Sheet Information System (BASIS), a PC-based set of integrated tools for budgeting, forecasting, and ALM.

Patten also called upon consultant George Darling for advice, a move that produced several "meaty, low-risk ideas that made sense and have definitely paid dividends," according to the Maine banker. They included the packaging and selling of mortgages and the securitization of assets, which helped protect Camden National's earnings as interest rates fell.

Securitization of mortgages is not a new phenomenon. As a strategy, it developed during the 1980s as a way of removing credit risk from the balance sheet. That feature made it particularly attractive to managers like John Bitner, senior vice president at Eastern Bank in Salem, Massachusetts. This institution has displayed its strength as a community bank and middle-market lender. In the latter half of the 1980s, the bank's asset size doubled to more than $1 billion.

Unlike Camden National, however, Eastern Bank has not been reticent about looking outside his bank's market domain for fresh funds. "By participating in the national CD market, (we can) raise deposits through brokers. It's an attractive option when there is a rate war going on in the local area," explained Bitner.

Striking a balance is the ultimate goal of all risk management, but fine-tuning to an individual bank's situation can be, as Bitner puts it, "as unique as a fingerprint." In mid-1990, Eastern Bank started using duration analysis software from Chase Financial Technologies called REALM. The program analyzes different interest-rate scenarios and their effect on both income and the market value of the bank's portfolio equity. See Table 11–1.

Chase Financial Technologies' duration analysis method is one of three that are now popularly used in ALM systems. The traditional "static gap" method measures the spread between current assets and liabilities and the current portfolio's sensitivity to interest rate movements. The simulated or dynamic gap approach takes the current book of business and simulates alternative business scenarios under different interest rate conditions. The result is a matrix of potential income generated from each of those possibilities.

Table 11–1.   REALM NII Sensitivity Matrix Reports
Periods 9008 to 9017

Scenario	Falling	Flat	Rising	Portfolio Income Range	Worst Case Exposure
Basecase	102,730	103,588	103,774	1,044	18,214
Increase Volume 10	111,856	111,069	108,863	2,993	12,081
Increase Volume 20	120,944	118,510	113,924	7,020	7,020

"A few years ago the banking industry didn't focus on duration," noted Mel Strauss, vice president of Chase Financial. "They're now more aware of duration as a technique and the need to look at market value of portfolios and equity. They have a better understanding of the math involved. Also, financial instruments have become more complex. Whereas, before, instruments were relatively simple. We now see coupon frequencies that may change, negative amortization, changing spreads, and imbedded options. Banks can input their own particular mix of instruments into ALM programs."

Banks become more liability-sensitive as rates drop and more asset-sensitive as rates rise. The trick is to anticipate possible or probable scenarios before it's too late or in time to minimize damage. Geoffrey Webb, director of research and development at Sendero in Scottsdale, Arizona, sees a clear distinction between planning and analytics. The latter can identify potential problems that elude planners. "Analytical tools provide ideas to optimze earnings and income under certain scenarios."

Analytical tools are features in Sendero's top-of-the-line ALM system *Model CS*, released in 1991. Another part of the CS package is detail planners, which give bankers the ability to create up to 1,600 different balance sheet item categories. "This way bankers can process information at a very detailed level and aggregate the results," Webb explained. "Conversely, once you know the aggregate you can make adjustments at the detail level."

Asset Sales, Pros And Cons

ALM experts agreed that asset sales are not a smart route to get better mileage out of a bank's operations. Most banks can't shrink operational costs to take advantage of smaller asset size. More importantly, banks in crisis situations get stuck selling their most valuable assets. In many cases, this effectively destroys the bank's long-term viability. Successful sales can hasten the deterioration of the balance sheet in many cases. "Asset sales put the bank in a liquidation mode," argued Darling. "Once you begin shedding assets you might as well give the keys to the bank to the FDIC."

There are, however, many instances where banks can use asset sales to focus the institution on its main businesses and areas of perceived opportunity. During Bank of America's dark year of 1986–1987, for example, the California bank sold about $24 billion in assets, including its world headquarters building in San Francisco, to plug the holes and forestall a takeover attempt by Southern California rival First Interstate Bank.

Cost control is critical in the drive to improve or fine-tune earnings. Some bankers mistakenly believe that large institutions are best able to squeeze out operating costs in economies of scale and scope. The truth is that small banks can do as good a job as their big bank brethren. Camden National's Patten spoke proudly of his bank's performance: "We have kept our operating expenses as a percent of assets at 70 basis points lower than our peer group."

One alternative for banks in a capital crunch is to "work your assets harder," according to Darling. Seek out ways to grow out of the problem in a constructive fashion. Regulators will listen to a well-reasoned plan that is supported by management commitment and a sound ALM strategy.

Regulators are happiest when they find a bank with high capital, high liquidity, and high income with minimal exposure and no credit risk. Few institutions measure up to the ideal. Regulators have certainly contributed to the surge of interest in analytics, even if banks object to the ways in which regulators ask to look at data, ways that, until now, banks and ALCOs have pretty much ignored.

There is a positive side effect of regulator scrutiny that few ALM managers appreciate. ALM was formerly a functional need within the bank, and getting management commitment and resources to do the job properly proved difficult. "Regulators have forced us to take ALM seriously. You could say that they have helped elevate ALM into a strategic, management role."

Another ongoing debate among ALM practitioners revolves around the question: Is ALM a science or an art? Those who argue for the former note that the models and systems to perform the analysis keep on improving. A deeper understanding of information and data requirements has increased sophistication. On the other hand, prophesizing can never be completely reduced to a formula. One also needs to know what lies behind the numbers and must rely on intangible factors like intuition and business gut feeling.

Simply put, banks are in the business of buying and selling money. New technologies and new techniques that assist in analyzing for productivity and profitability arm bankers to wage the battle in modern style against age-old competitors as well as nonbank contenders.

Subject Index

Page numbers followed by f refer to illustrations,
page numbers followed by a t refer to tables.

A

Accounts per household, 11f, 11-12
Adaptive Information Systems, and
    image integration, 100-101
ALADDIN system, 58
Alliances between banks, 48-49
Alpha, 17t
*Analyzing Success and Failure in Banking
    Consolidation*, 2
Animated cartoon/special effects
    infatuation, and
    presentation graphics, 73
Asset liability management, 206-211
    asset sales and, 210
    cost control and, 210-211
    main elements of, 207-208
    regulation and, 211
Augmented product, 14-15
Autodialing, 101
Automated clearing house, 190
Automated Service Machine, 185
Automated teller machines, 83-91
    Fleet/Norstar and, 88
    history of, 83-84
    leaders in, 88-90, 89t
    and modifying customer behaviors,
      87-88
    promotions involving, 88
    smart marketing of, 86
    transaction mix, 85, 85f
    usage trends, 84t, 85

Automated voice response, 92-102
    advantages of, 95-96
    autodialing, 101
    Automatic Number Identification,
      101
    caller profile, 92
    Chase Manhattan Bank and, 100
    Chemical Bank and, 99
    Citibank and, 99
    and deregulation of telephone
      industry, 94
    Fidelity Investments and, 93
    First Union Bank and, 93-94
    Hollywood Federal and, 96
    and home banking, 94-95
    and image integration, 100-101
    as information servers, 100-101
    Interest Checking, 18t
    Interest rate risk, 207
    market for, 93
    operating features, 97
    predictions regarding, 101-102
    and speech synthesis, 94
    Syntellect Inc. and, 94
    and touch tone phones, 94
    trends in, 97-98
    uses of, 98
    voice technology, 93-94
    Wells Farge Bank and, 98-99
Automatic Number Identification, 101

B

Baby boomers, 20-22
Backfile conversions, and image
    processing, 119
Balance Sheet Information System, 208
BankAmerica Systems Engineering,
    197
Banking Modem, 192
BANKMATCH, 33
Bank product bundling. *See* Bundling
Banks without walls, 182-185
    Automated Service Machine, 185
    FirstDirect Bank, 183-184
    Key Bank and, 182-183
    technology and, 184-185
Behavioral research, and branch bank
    merchandising, 163-164
Blue Max, 17t
Branch Analyzer, 202-203
Branchbanker, 72
Branch bank merchandising, 157-174
    arranging environment, 164,166
    Banc One and, 168-169
    bank retailing, 158-162
    behavioral research and, 163-164
    Citibank and, 171
    communication and, 163
    consultants and, 173
    deregulation and, 157
    downsizing, 169
    Envirosell research and, 163-164,
        165f
    furniture and, 171
    future trends, 168-171
    as media centers, 163
    Money Access Center Network, 169-
        170
    planning and, 172
    Que and Teller Management
        System, 172, 173f
    self-service technology, 169-170
    strategic shopping and, 167-168
    traditional banking values and, 172
    video and media, 167
Branchless banking. *See* Banks without
    walls
Bundling, 16-19, 17t-18t

C

CASE technology, 40

Huntington National Bank and, 40-
    41
Cash Dispatch system, 62
Change, openness to, 3-4
Check processing, 115-117
    First Interstate Bank of Washington
        and, 117
    Mellon Bank and, 117
    savings and, 118
ChemPlus, 16
Chief Information Officer, role of, 47
Cincinnati Business Information
    Systems, 116
CIS information systems, 128
Citi-One, 17
CitiShopper, 15
Classic, 18t
Color graphics, and product presenta-
    tion, 72
Communication, importance with
    customer, 5, 28-29
Communication networks, 190-193
    automated clearing house, 190
    First Union Bank and, 191-192
    multiplexers, 192-193
    Security Pacific Bank and, 191
    T-1 networks, 191
    very small aperture terminals, 192
Compact teller terminal, 56
COMPASS, 125-126
*Competitive Strategy: Techniques for
    Analyzing Industries
    and Competitors*, 47
Computer Aided Teller Scheduling
    system, 172
Connectivity, 6
Consumer loans, and automation, 114-
    115
Continuity banking, 27
Convenience, customer, 5
CORPMATCH, 33
Cost control, and asset liability
    management, 210-211
Credit cards, expert systems and, 186-
    187
Credit risk, 207
Critical mass
    Citicorp and, 15
    and retail strategy, 15
    Valley National Bank and, 15
Cross-selling, 12, 124, 141, 141f, 150
Cue card syndrome, 73

Cultural imperatives, 4
Currency dispensing devices, 62-64
Customer business, banks percentage
    of, 13
Customer confidence in retail banking,
    3
Customer information files
    aging, 34
    assessing, 4
    and banking goals, 32
    common problems in, 33-34
    dirty data, 33
    householding, 36-38
    integration barriers, 34-35
    laundering of, 33-34
    and marketing, 37
    marketing systems, 127-130
        Customer Development Corpora-
        tion and, 127
        Okra Marketing Corporation and,
        128
        PC-based, 130
        Peoples Savings Bank and, 129
        Security Pacific Bank and, 128
    search methods, 34
Customer information resources,
    Norwest Corporation and, 37
Customerized banking, 4-5
Customer satisfaction testing, First
    Union Corporation and,
    28
Customer service, definition of, 27-28
Customer service representatives. *See
    also* Platform automation
    and continuity banking, 27
    and presentation graphics, 73
    product knowledge, 71
    role, 67
    sample of platform activity, 70f
    skills required, 69-70

D
Database marketing, 131-133
    American Savings Bank and, 132
    Chase Manhattan Bank and, 131-132
    Claritas Corporation and, 132
    Equifax Marketing Decision Systems
        and, 132-133

    Premier Bancorp and, 133
    segmentation and, 131
Debit cards, and point of sale strate-
    gies. *See* Direct debit
    point of sale
Demand deposit accounting system, 38
Depository Institutions Deregulation
    and Monetary Control
    Act, 157
Deregulation, 157
Direct debit point of sale, 102-106
    benefit of, 102-103
    and bottom line, 102
    fee income and, 104-105
    leaders in, 106t
    as regional phenomena, 103
    supermarkets and, 103, 103t, 104t
    terminals and transaction data, 105t
    weighing risks, 105-106
Direct marketing, 134
    Midlantic Bank and, 134
DocuBanc, 117
Document design, and image process-
    ing, 118
Documents, automated. *See* Image
    processing
Duplex banking, 171
Dynamic growth, Baxter Credit Union
    and, 29

E
Electronic signature verification, 61-62
Environment, and branch bank
    merchandising, 164, 166
Expected product, 14
Expense control, and information
    systems, 45
Expert systems, 186-190
    areas for consideration, 189-190
    caveats for, 189
    and credit cards, 187-188
    and loan review, 186-187
    Oak Hills Saving and Loan and, 188-
    189
    personal financial advisor systems,
    188
    size of application and, 188
    Star Bank and, 187-188
    Trustee Savings Bank and, 188

F

Fee income, and direct debit point of sale, 104-105
Financial analysis, and platform automation, 74-75
Financial Connections, 17t-18t
Financial industry providers, perceived positions of, 30f
Fortysomething customers, 22-23
Furniture, 171

G

GAIN, 126
Garn-St. Germain Depository Institutions Act, 157
Generic product, 14
Genesis, 128
Glass-Steagall Act, 1

H

Harte-Hanks Data Technologies, 34
Historical performance data, 46
Home banking, and interactive voice response, 94-95
Householding, 36-38
Hybrid products, 15

I

Identity, bank, 10-19
  bank-customer relationships, 10
  industry statistical comparison, 10-16
  product bundling, 16-19
ImageBanc, 116
Image integration, and interactive voice response, 100-101
ImagePlus High-Performance Transaction System, 117
Image processing, 107-121
  American Express and, 115
  backfile conversions, 119
  checking, 115-117
  and consumer loans, 114-115
  departmental documents, 110-111

department candidates for, 118
  document design and, 118
  Eastern Heights State Bank and, 111
  electronic bottlenecks, 114
  first encounters with, 108
  future automated documents, 113
  lost documents, 109
  and mortgage lending, 111-112
  optical disk storage systems, 109
  paper bottlenecks, 109
  productivity and, 119
  retraining staffs, 118
  rules for, 120-121
  testing, 119
Incentive programs, and sales, 147-150
  automating, 150
  cross-selling bonuses, 150
  Pacific First Bank and, 149
  Washington Mutual Savings Bank and, 148
InfoImage Item Processing, 116
Information access, improving, 47
Information battleground, 44-47
Information systems, maintenance of, 38-43
  budget, 38
  prepackaged solutions, 41-43
  reverse engineering, 40
  software improvement, 39
Innovative Systems, Inc., 33-34
Integrated document preparation, Valley Banks and, 110
Integrated marketing. *See* Database marketing
Integration barriers, and customer service files, 34-35
Interactive voice response. *See* Automated voice response.
Interactive Platform Machines, 91
Interest Checking, 18t
Interest rate risk, 207

J

Japanese Post Office Savings System, and automated teller machines, 90
Judgement Processor, 187

L
Leadership for Quality, 19
LINK products, 192
Liquidity risk, 207-208
Loan automation, Perpetual Savings Bank, 114-115
Loan review, expert systems and, 186-187

M
Mail banking, 182-185
Maintenance of information systems, 38-43
Management commitment to change, 6
Management Information Control Systems, Banc One and, 46
Manager Information Systems, role of, 47
Marketing, 123-138
    analyzing competition, 125-127
    BankSource and, 126
    cross-selling existing customers, 124
    customer benefits, 136
    customer information files and, 127-130
    database, 131-133
    direct contact, 134
    Donnelly Marketing Information Services and, 126
    focus of, 137
    goal of, 123
    market research, 125
    Perpetual Savings Bank and, 125-126
    self-rank study, 124
    telemarketing, 134-136
    Urban Science Applications Inc. and, 126
    weak links in, 136-137
Marketing File Access System, 127
Marshall & Ilsley Data Services, 42-43
Master Financial System, 41-42
MAXIM software, 61
"McBanking" phenomenon, 3-4
Media, and branch bank merchandising, 167
MicroMarketer, 128
MicroVISION, 21-22
Money Access Center Network, 169-170
Mortgage lending and automation, 111-112
    Marquette Bank and, 112

Mortgages, securitization of, 208
Mortgage Vision, 186
Motivation in sales, 151
Motivator sales and management system, 146-147

N
NCR Teller Assisted Automation, 63-64
New accounts, opening of, 13
    and platform automation, 68

O
Office equipment, 171
OneLine multiplexer, 192-193
OnePlus, 16
Optical disk storage systems, 109

P
Paper bottlenecks, and information processing, 109
Paycheck cashing machines, 91
Performance reward, sales, 147-150
PIN systems, 88
Platform automation, 67-82
    Bank of America and, 79-80, 81
    Bank South and, 71
    capturing customer information, 71
    and financial analysis, 74-75
    Fleet/Norstar Services Company and, 77-78
    Mellon Bank and, 79
    presentation graphics, 71-73
        pitfalls, 73
    primary attributes, 68-69
    Pugent Sound National Bank and, 72
    record keeping and ticklers, 74
    reviewing performance of, 75-77
    sales tools, 77
    Shawmut National Corporation and, 78
    Valley Bancorporation, 76
Point of sale strategies, and debit cards. *See* Direct debit point of sale
Potential product, 15

Presentation graphics, and platform automation, 71-73
Prime Advantage program, 26
PRIZM segments, 134, 135f
Product-based banking, compared to relationship-based banking, 14
Product grouping, Mellon Bank and, 19
Productivity, 195-202
  Bank of America model, 196-199
    Alpha and, 198-199
    and applications architecture, 197-198
    centralization and, 198
    consolidation and, 198
    staff reduction, 199
  Branch Banking & Trust Company and, 205
  data on, 195-196
  Electronic Data Systems and, 204
  Fleet/Norstar Financial Group model, 199-202
    consolidation, 202
    matrix system of responsibility, 201
    senior management involvement, 201-202
  gaps and profitability, 204-205
  Norwest Bank and, 204-205
Product linkage, and customer information files, 34
Product ownership statistics, customer, 12, 12f
PROFILE core banking system, 35, 36f
PROFILE marketing workstation, 130
Profitability, 202-206. *See also* Productivity; Risk Management
  analyzing for, 202-203
  Branch Analyzer, 203-204
  and customer relationships, 205-206
  and productivity gaps, 204-205
Promotions, involving automated teller machines, 88

Q
Que and Teller Management System, 172, 173f

R
REALM, 209, 209f

Recognition Equipment Inc., 116
Record keeping, and platform automation, 74
Re-engineering, information system, 39
Relationship banking, 9-30
  categorizing customers, 19-27
  compared to product-based banking, 14
  identification in marketplace, 10-19
  providing quality service, 27-30
Relationship packaging, 16
  Chemical Bank and, 16
Retail merchandising, 158-162
  Dollar Dry Dock Bank and, 160-162
  environment of, 158-159
Retaining customers, 29-30
Retirement planning, 23-24
Retraining staff, and image processing, 118
Reverse engineering, information system, 40
Risk management, 206-211
  Camden National Bank and, 208
  Chase Financial Technologies and, 209-210
  Eastern Bank and, 208-209
  Sendero and, 210

S
Sales, 139-155
  confusion with marketing, 140
  cross-selling, 12, 124, 141, 141t, 150
  establishing sales culture, 140, 142
  low staff morale and, 142-143
  measuring current level, 144-145
  motivation, 151
  productivity tools, 145-146
  reporting systems, 143-147
  rewarding performance, 147-150
  training, 151-155
Sales Challenge, 153
SalesExpert, 146
Sales reporting systems
  American Savings Bank and, 144
  automation and, 143-144
  Motivator, 146-147
  SalesExpert program, 146
  San Diego Trust and Savings Bank and, 146

Sales reporting systems (cont'd)
    Trackstar, 145
    $uccess, 146
Satellite television, and sales training,
    154
Savings and loan crisis, 1
Securitization of mortgages, 208
Select Banking, 16
SellScreen, 72
Senior citizens, 25-26
    Society National Bank and, 26
    Valley National Bank and, 26
Senior Partners, 17t
Service quality, 27-30
Services per household, 11f, 11-12
Single service useage, 11f, 11-12, 13f
SMART account, 19
Software improvement, and informa-
    tion systems, 39
Sorter and Loader, 62
Speech synthesis, and interactive voice
    response, 94
Staff morale, and turnover, 142-143
Standard Account Type Table, 188-189
Structural changes, 48
Student Plus, 16
Supermarket branching, 177f, 177-182
    design and construction costs, 180
    drawbacks, 179
    marketing tactics, 180-181
    National Commerce
        Bankcorporation, 178
    staffing, 180
    Wells Fargo Bank, 178-179
Supermarkets, and direct debit point
    of sale, 103, 103t, 104t
Superregional retail banking trend, 3-4
Syntellect, and image integration, 100-
    101

T
Telebanking. See Automated voice
    response
TeleLoan, 114-115
Telemarketing, 134-136
    First Interstate Bank of California
        and, 133-136
    Perpetual Savings Bank and, 136
Telephone industry deregulation, and
    interactive voice response, 94

Teller automation, 54-60. See also
    Automated teller machines
    cash dispensing devices, 62-64
    Chemical Bank and, 64-65
    CoreStates Financial Corporation
        and, 53
    goals of, 55-56
    most desirable features, 59
    optimum mix of, 65-66
    PC-based, 56-57
    Twin City Federal Savings Bank
        and, 62
    Valley Bancorporation and, 58
Teller Cash Input, 62
Teller system automation. See also
    Teller automation
    average teller transaction activity,
        52f
    description of, 51-52
    performance, 51
    PNC Financial Corporation and, 60-
        61
The College Savings Plan, 15
The Marketing Imagination, 14-15
Ticklers, and platform automation, 74
T-1 networks, 191
Total Customer Service: The Ultimate
    Weapon, 27
TotalMarketer, 128
Trackstar, 145
Training, sales, 151-155
    Bankers Trust and, 154
    Bank of America and, 152
    Chase Lincoln First Bank of Roches-
        ter and, 152
    computer-based, 152
    interactive videodisks, 152-154
    motivation, 151
    satellite television and, 154
    Wells Fargo Bank and, 152
Transaction mix, and automated teller
    machines, 85, 85f

V
ValuAdded, 18t
Vboss operations, 76
Very small aperture terminals, 192
Video, and branch bank merchandis-
    ing, 167

Videodisks, interactive, and sales
    training, 152-154
  Sales Challenge, 153
Viewstar, 113
VISION market segmentation, 132, 133

W

WORM optical disk storage systems,
  109

Y

Youth appeal, Dollar Dry Dock
  Savings Bank, 24-25

Bank and Company Index

Page numbers followed by t refer to tables.

A
Adaptive Information Systems, 100
Alaska USA FCU, 106t
America First Credit Union, 92
American Express, 115
American Savings Bank, 132, 144
Ameritrust Corp., 103, 106t
Ampersand Corporation, 72

B
Banc One, 3, 17t, 46, 95, 103, 106t, 168
Bankers Trust, 42, 154
Bank of America, 17t, 78, 79, 81, 89t, 152, 196-199
Bank of Bermuda, 35
Bank of Boston, 89
Bank of Montreal, 42
Bank South, 64, 71, 106
Barnett Banks, 17t
Baxter Credit Union, 29
BayBanks, 18t, 89-90, 89t
Branch Banking & Trust Company, 205

C
Camden National Bank, 208
Central Trust Co., 106t

Chase Financial Technologies, 209-210
Chase Lincoln First Bank, 152
Chase Manhattan Bank, 15, 42, 95, 100, 101, 131
Chemical Bank, 16, 64, 75, 99, 113
Chevy Chase Federal Savings Bank, 186
Chizek & Company, 172
Citibank, 15, 17t, 88, 89t, 99, 119, 130, 171
City National Bank, 57, 62
Claritas Corporation, 132, 134
Cogensys, 186
Commonwealth Mortgage Corporation, 112
Computrol Inc., 39
CoreStates Financial Corp., 53, 63, 86
Credit Management Solutions Inc., 114
Customer Development Corporation, 127

D
Davenport Bank & Trust, 106
Dierbergs, 104
Dollar Dry Dock Savings Bank, 24-25, 160-162
Donnelly Marketing Information Services, 126

E
Earnings Performance Group, 203-204
Eastern Bank, 208
Eastern Heights State Bank, 111
Electronic Data Systems, 204
Envirosell Inc., 163
Equifax Marketing Decision Systems, 132-133
Exchange National Bank, 109

F
Ferguson & Company, 126
Fidelity Investments, 10, 93
Fifth Third Bank, 106t, 179
FileNet Corp., 116
FirstDirect Bank, 183
First International Bank of Washington, 117
First Interstate Bank, 89t, 135
First National Bank, 56, 182
First Tennessee Bank, 106t
First Union Bank, 28, 89t, 93, 146-147, 191-192
Fleet/Norstar, 77, 86-87, 88, 89, 199-202
Florida National Bank, 89t

G
Gallagher Financial Systems, 112
GTE EFT Services, 88

H
Harte-Hanks Data Technologies, 34, 128
Hollywood Federal, 96
Household Finance, 10
Huntington National Bank, 40-41

I
Indiana National Bank, 33
Innovative Microsystems, 146
Innovative Systems Inc., 33-34
International Business Machines, 117
ISC-Bunker Ramo, 170

K
Key Bank USA, 182

L
Language Technology, 39
Learning International, 153

M
Management Science Associates Inc., 130
Manning Professional Services, 145
Marine Midland Bank, 126
Marquette Bank, 112
Marshall & Isley Data Services, 42-43
Mellon Bank, 19, 38, 79, 117, 179
Midlantic Bank, 134

N
National Commerce Bankcorporation, 178
NationsBank, 3, 17t
Network EFT, 88, 89t
Northern Trust, 42
Northwest Bank, 18t
Norwest Bank, 16, 37, 48, 204-205

O
Oak Hills Saving and Loan, 188
Okra Marketing Corporation, 128
Olympics Savings Bank, 179

P
Pacific Bank of Washington, 91
Pacific First Bank, 148
PA Consulting Group, 176
Paradyne, 192
Peoples Savings Bank, 129
Perle System, 192
Perpetual Savings Bank, 114, 125t, 136
Personal Financial Assistant Inc., 185
PNC Financial Corp., 60-61
Premier Bancorp, 133

Provident National Bank, 54, 80
Publix Super Markets, 106t
Puget Sound National Bank, 72, 77

R
Recognition Equipment Inc., 116
Resource One, 146, 150
Rocky Mountain Bank, 89t

S
Sacramento Savings and Loan, 204
Sanchez Computer Associates, 35
San Diego Trust and Savings Bank, 146
Santa Barbara National Bank, 26
Security Pacific, 16, 18t, 42, 89t, 106t,
    128, 191
Sendero, 210
Shared Financial Systems, 193
Shawmut National Corp., 78
Society National Bank, 26
Southern Belle Bank, 94
Sovran Financial Corporation, 153
Star Bank, 187
Steelcase, 171
SunGard Financial System, 208
Syntellect Inc., 94, 100

T
Texas Bank of Commerce, 65

Timeplex, 192
Trustee Savings Bank, 188
Twin City Federal Savings Bank, 62

U
Union Bank, 56, 96
Unisys, 116
Urban Science Applications Inc., 126

V
Valley Bancorporation, 58, 76
Valley Bank, 85, 110
Valley National Bank, 15, 26, 76, 171

W
Wachovia Bank and Trust, 102
Washington Mutual Savings Bank, 148
Wells Fargo Bank, 89t, 98, 106t, 152,
    178
Wilmington Trust, 75, 88

X
Xerox, 144

Printed in the United States
22102LVS00001B/143